THREE
PHILOSOPHICAL
DIALOGUES

ANSELM

THREE PHILOSOPHICAL DIALOGUES

On Truth
On Freedom of Choice
On the Fall of the Devil

Translated, with Introduction and Notes, by
Thomas Williams

Hackett Publishing Company, Inc.
Indianapolis/Cambridge

Copyright © 2002 by Hackett Publishing Company, Inc.

15 14 13 12 11 10   2 3 4 5 6 7 8

For further information, please address:
  Hackett Publishing Company, Inc.
  P.O. Box 44937
  Indianapolis, IN 46244-0937

  www.hackettpublishing.com

Cover design by Listenberger Design & Associates

Library of Congress Cataloging-in-Publication Data

Anselm, Saint, Archbishop of Canterbury, 1033–1109.
  [Dialogues. English. Selections]
  Three philosophical dialogues / Anselm; translated, with introduction
and notes, by Thomas Williams
    p. cm.
  Includes index.
  Contents: On truth—On freedom of choice—On the fall of the Devil.
  ISBN 0-87220-612-2 (cloth)—ISBN 0-87220-611-4 (paper)
    1. Free will and determinism. 2. Truth. 3. Devil. 4. Philosophy,
Medieval. I. Williams, Thomas, 1967– II. Title.
  B765.A81 .A2513 2002
  189'.4—dc21   2001051549

ISBN-13: 978-0-87220-612-0 (cloth)
ISBN-13: 978-0-87220-611-3 (pbk.)

CONTENTS

NOTE ON THE TRANSLATION

The Latin text translated here is the critical edition of F. S. Schmitt in *S. Anselmi Cantuariensis Archiepiscopi Opera Omnia* (Stuttgart-Bad Canstatt: Friedrich Fromann Verlag, 1968), I:169–376. At p. 251, l. 15 (in the last sentence of the teacher's last speech in *DCD* 11), I have followed manuscript Q against the editor and read "dicuntur de eo". Otherwise I have followed the editor.

References are given to the dialogues by the abbreviations of their Latin names, as follows:

> *DV* = *On Truth* (*De veritate*)
> *DLA* = *On Freedom of Choice* (*De libertate arbitrii*)
> *DCD* = *On the Fall of the Devil* (*De casu diaboli*)

An asterisk in the text indicates that the word so marked is explained in the Glossary. I have generally marked such terms only on their first occurrence in a chapter and in passages where their use seems especially likely to cause misunderstanding. Occasionally the same speaker who ends one chapter begins the next. In such cases, the new chapter begins without an indication of the speaker.

INTRODUCTION

If you asked me, or just about any other scholar familiar with Anselm's work, what the three dialogues translated here are *about*, you would probably be told that they are all three about topics in *metaphysics*, with some ethics thrown in as well. *On Truth* concerns the nature of truth, a metaphysical topic, although it also discusses the nature of justice, an ethical topic. *On Freedom of Choice* and *On the Fall of the Devil* both focus on the nature, extent, and exercise of free will, again metaphysical topics, with a considerable emphasis on the purpose of free will, an ethical topic. But when *Anselm* described these dialogues in his Preface, he called them "three treatises pertaining to the study of Holy Scripture." Now either Anselm and his modern readers have entirely different ideas about what's important in these dialogues, or else they have entirely different ideas about what it means for something to pertain to the study of Scripture—or perhaps both. The matter deserves a close look, since if Anselm is doing something other than what we naturally take him to be doing, we will risk grave misunderstanding if we don't try to understand what exactly that is. (Of course, we may decide in the end that what's interesting about Anselm's discussion in these dialogues is not what *he* thinks is interesting. But we should want to know whether we are reading Anselm on his own terms or using Anselm to pursue our own independent interests.)

So we have two questions before us. First, does Anselm mean something different from what we would mean in saying that these dialogues pertain to the study of Holy Scripture? And second, are the discussions that modern readers find central to these dialogues entirely different from the ones that Anselm thought were central? I will begin by answering the first question, explaining what Anselm has in mind when he says that these dialogues pertain to the study of Holy Scripture. Now even if you're not reading these dialogues because you're interested in Scripture (and given our present-day curricular divisions, the odds are that you're reading them because you're interested in *philosophy*), you should keep reading, because the philosophical payoff will come surprisingly soon. It will turn out that Anselm has in mind something quite different from what we think of as biblical exegesis, something that will look far more like philosophy. Then I will proceed to the second question. In that connection I will suggest that Anselm is interested in precisely the same discussions that interest modern philosophical readers: that is, in the discussion of metaphysical and ethical issues. But he may not be interested in them for quite the same reasons that some modern readers are, and his reasons for engaging in those discussions are as important to the character of his thinking as the positions he defends.

We can begin by taking a look at the opening line of *On the Fall of the Devil*:

> When the Apostle [Paul] says "What do you have that you did not receive?": is he saying this only to human beings, or to angels as well?

Now contemporary biblical scholars would look at this question and roll their eyes. "Paul certainly isn't speaking to angels in this passage," they would protest; "he's not even speaking to all human beings. He's writing to first-century Christians in the new church at Corinth, and he's admonishing them not to boast about their spiritual gifts. That's why, after asking 'What do you have that you did not receive?' he continues by asking 'Why then do you boast as if you have not received?' The answer Paul expects to his first question is, obviously, *Nothing*. Since the Corinthians have nothing they have not received from God, they ought not to preen themselves on their spiritual gifts as if they were somehow responsible for them." And so, the contemporary biblical scholar might conclude, asking whether these words are addressed to angels is just plain silly.

If Anselm could be brought into this debate, he would surely retort that the critic's reasoning, if it works at all, proves far too much. For none of Scripture—not one word of it—was written for an audience of people like you and me: educated English speakers of the early twenty-first century. If the critic's reasoning is right, then, the question "What do you have that you have not received?" is not asked of *us* either. And yet that is in fact an entirely apt question, and one whose answer is of great theological and philosophical importance. Suppose that literally everything we have—every desire, every choice, every virtue, every emotion, every talent—is received entirely from God. Then it becomes very hard to see why we should get any credit at all for whatever good things we do ("Why then do you boast as if you had not received?") and any blame for whatever evil we do. Wouldn't God bear all the responsibility for both good and evil?

Of course, this is a problem only if we have some reason to think that everything we have is received from God. But Anselm believes we have ample reason to think so. Not only does Scripture affirm it, but reason shows it. In both the *Monologion* and the *Proslogion* Anselm argues that God is the ultimate source of everything that is. And in chapter 5 of *On Truth* he argues (in effect) that no matter how things are, they are that way because God directs them to be that way. Nothing can be otherwise than as God, the Supreme Truth, directs. In other words, purely philosophical reflection shows that God is, in a very strong sense, the final and complete answer to every question of the form "Why is *x* the way it is?"

So Paul's question to the Corinthians seems to imply that they have nothing but what they have received from God, and rational reflection backs up that implication. And yet both Scripture and rational reflection also tell us that God punishes people, and it seems unjust for God to punish people for failing to make good choices if those good choices can come only from God. God seems to withhold goodness from people and then punish them for lacking it. So there is an urgent theological and philosophical need to figure out how widely Paul's question is meant to apply.

Still, why *angels*? How does it help our philosophical problem to investigate the application of Paul's question to angels instead of asking the (presumably easier) question about its application to human beings? The answer, I think, is that the case of angels excludes a number of complications that are extraneous to Anselm's main interest. Anselm tells us elsewhere (in *De concordia* 1.6) that in these dialogues he is concerned with freedom only to the extent that freedom bears on salvation. Human beings at least seem to have freedom that has no salvific significance at all: my eternal destiny does not hang on what I choose to have for dinner tonight, though that choice does seem to be free. Rather than being distracted by questions about whether I really do have such freedom, and whether, if I do, that freedom is the same sort of freedom I employ in making the choices that *do* matter for eternity, Anselm asks about the angels. For all we know about angelic freedom is that some angels fell and others didn't. The ones who fell are no longer capable of doing good; the ones who stayed firm are no longer capable of doing evil. So with the angels we get exactly one choice, and that choice clearly does matter for the angels' eternal destiny.

There is another reason for focusing on angels. Human beings are, according to the Christian doctrine of the Fall, damaged goods in need of divine repair. Those who have been repaired are clearly not entitled to boast of their restored condition, since it was God who repaired them; for we are, according to the doctrine of the Fall, too damaged to repair ourselves. God's repair work is known in theology as "grace," and the problem of the relationship between grace and human freedom is a notoriously messy one. The question of grace does not arise for the angels, however, because the angels were all in their original pristine condition when they made their primal choice. So if Paul's question does apply to the angels, it can't be about grace. It must instead be about whether that one primal choice—the choice by which the good angels remained obedient to God and the evil angels fell—was something received from God or not. If it was, we must explain how it could be just for God to hold the evil angels responsible for a choice that they received from him; if it was not, we must explain how God can be the source of all things when he's not the source of the angels' choice.

The upshot of all this is that philosophical reflection is necessary if we are to understand what Paul was getting at when he asked the Corinthians, "What do you have that you did not receive?" Such philosophical reflection therefore "pertains to the study of Holy Scripture." It now becomes much easier to see why Anselm described all three of these dialogues as pertaining to the study of Holy Scripture. *On Truth* begins by noticing that we speak of God as Truth. Now that's Scriptural language: Jesus identifies himself as the Truth in John 14:6, and 1 John 5:6 identifies the Spirit as Truth.[1] If we are to understand this Scriptural language, we have to figure out what it could mean to speak of God as Truth. Is this our ordinary use of 'truth', as when we speak of the truth of a statement or an opinion? And if it is, how can the Truth that is God be connected with the truth that statements and opinions have? Furthermore, Jesus speaks of "doing the truth" in

---

1. In Anselm's translation of the Bible, however, this verse says that the Spirit testifies that Christ is the Truth.

John 3:21, so there must also be truth in actions. But what could that be? And how is it connected to the truth of statements, on the one hand, and the Truth that is God, on the other? These are some of the key questions that Anselm raises in *On Truth*. They are philosophical questions, but they pertain to the study of Holy Scripture because their aim is to clarify the meaning of the language used in Scripture. In the same vein, one important line of argument in *On Freedom of Choice* is intended to elucidate the scriptural claim that "he who commits sin is a slave to sin" (John 8:34). For it would seem that if someone can be enslaved by sin, he is weaker than sin or somehow subject to its power. And then what becomes of freedom and moral responsibility? Here again, in order to understand what Scripture is saying, we are driven to ask philosophical questions.

So one thing Anselm meant by describing these dialogues as "treatises pertaining to the study of Holy Scripture" is that they are devoted to elucidating scriptural language through rational argument. But I think he had something else in mind as well. It is not only the content of these dialogues but also their *method* that pertains to the study of Holy Scripture. Anselm's most characteristic method in these dialogues is the analysis of language. A good illustration of the sort of procedure he uses can be found in chapter 5 of *On Truth*, where Anselm tries to understand what Jesus means in John 3:21 when he says that "He who does the truth comes to the light." What could the truth of actions be? Anselm first notes the contrasting claim in John 3:20: "He who does evil hates the light." He then reasons as follows:

> If doing evil and doing the truth are opposites, as the Lord indicates by saying that "He who does evil hates the light" and "He who does the truth comes to the light," then doing the truth is the same as doing good, since doing good and doing evil are contraries. Therefore, if doing the truth and doing good are both opposed to the same thing, they have the same signification.

So Anselm's first conclusion is about the signification (that is, roughly, the *meaning*) of "doing the truth": it means the same as "doing good."

Then he gives a separate analysis for both 'doing' and 'truth' individually. First, he explains what 'truth' means—or, in other words, what the truth of action is:

Now everyone agrees that those who do what they ought, do good and act correctly.[2] From this it follows that to act correctly is to do the truth, since it is agreed that to do the truth is to do good, and to do good is to act correctly. So nothing is more obvious than that the truth of action is its rectitude.

The truth of an action is its rectitude: that is, an action is true when it is 'right', when it is as it ought to be. The only thing left now for a full understanding of what is meant by "doing the truth," i.e., acting rightly, is to know what should count as 'doing', i.e., what constitutes 'acting'. Anselm explains:

> Now when the Lord said that "He who does the truth comes to the light," he meant us to take 'do' not just to mean what is properly* called doing, but as substituting for any verb. After all, he is not excluding from this truth or light someone who undergoes persecution "for righteousness' sake" [Matthew 5:10], or who is when and where he ought to be, or who stands or sits when he ought to, and so forth. No one says that such people are not doing good. And when the Apostle [Paul] says that everyone will receive a recompense "according to his deeds" [2 Corinthians 5:10], we should understand him to mean whatever we customarily identify as doing good or doing evil.

So Anselm concludes that the 'do' in 'do the truth' applies very broadly. I can "do" the truth even when I'm not *doing* anything, but instead undergoing what someone else is doing to me.

One common move in Anselm's analysis of scriptural language is his appeal to ordinary usage. In the present context, the student immediately goes on to note that

> Ordinary language, too, uses 'to do' both of undergoing and of many other things that are not doings. Hence, if I am not mistaken, we can also include among right actions an upright will, whose truth we investigated earlier, before the truth of action.

And the teacher replies:

> You are not mistaken. For someone who wills what he ought to is said to act correctly and to do good; nor is he excluded from those who do the truth.

2. "Act correctly" is literally "do rectitude."

The appeal to ordinary language does two things here. For one, it allows Anselm to tie this discussion of the truth of action to his previous discussion of the truth of willing. Willing is just a kind of action, so the truth of willing must be exactly the same thing as the truth of action. Since Anselm's purpose in *On Truth* is to argue that there is one truth in all true things, this is an important result.

The second purpose of the appeal to ordinary language is to assure us that in interpreting the language of Scripture, Anselm has not distorted its meaning. Such assurance is not especially urgent in the present case, since there's nothing terribly controversial about supposing that Jesus meant 'do' quite broadly when he spoke of "doing the truth." But sometimes the assurance that Anselm's interpretation of scriptural language has an analogue in ordinary language is sorely needed. For sometimes Anselm rejects what might seem the obvious meaning of a passage on the grounds that such a superficial interpretation would give the passage a meaning that we can show is just plain false. When this is the case, Anselm wants to assure the reader that he is not just playing with words, stretching the meaning of a passage beyond recognition. Rather, the meaning he finds there is one that we can find in our ordinary language. This is not to say that ordinary language is the ultimate court of appeal. Anselm acknowledges in chapter 12 of *On the Fall of the Devil* that

> Many things are said improperly in ordinary speech; but when it is incumbent upon us to search out the heart of the truth, we must remove the misleading impropriety to the greatest extent possible and as much as the subject matter demands.

But removing the imprecisions of ordinary language is as much a part of scriptural exegesis as it is of philosophical analysis, since—as Anselm often shows—Scripture uses the same imprecise, but philosophically clarifiable, ordinary language that we use in other contexts.

So these dialogues are aptly described as "pertaining to the study of Holy Scripture" not only because their metaphysical and ethical *content* serves the aim of clarifying the meaning of certain key passages of Scripture, but also because their *method* is the style of linguistic analysis that Anselm uses in studying Scripture. The answer to our first question—why Anselm describes these dialogues as he does—is therefore clear. And along the way the answer to our second question—whether what Anselm finds to be of interest in these dialogues matches what modern readers find to be of interest—has already begun to emerge. The metaphysical and ethical discussions that modern philosophical readers find most engaging are precisely the same discussions that Anselm took to be the central focus of these works. But what motivates Anselm's interest in those philosophical issues need not be the same thing that motivates the interest of contemporary readers. A contemporary reader might be interested in freedom, for example, because of its apparent connection with moral responsibility. Anselm is interested in freedom because it poses difficulties in understanding how the choices of God's creatures are related to the sovereign will of the Creator.

This does not mean that one must share Anselm's theological convictions in order to find these dialogues philosophically useful. *On the Fall of the Devil*, for example, contains a great deal of first-rate philosophy that is worth thinking about even if one doesn't believe in a devil or a Fall. But it's important to keep in mind that Anselm is not always addressing precisely the same questions that we would be asking in his place. So while it's often perfectly legitimate to detach his arguments from their intended purpose and put them to use in answering our own philosophical questions, we have to realize that that's what we're doing, and make the necessary adjustments. That is, we can use the techniques and arguments we find in the dialogues to develop Anselmian answers even to non-Anselmian questions.

On the other hand, understanding Anselm on his own terms (as opposed to using him as a resource for our independent philosophical purposes) has a great value as well, and part of the purpose of this introduction has been to enable you to understand Anselm in this way by explaining the purposes behind the arguments he puts forward in these dialogues and the analytical techniques he employs there. Entering sympathetically into Anselm's thought—looking at the philosophical problems through his eyes, with his aims in mind—can reveal new options, new ways of posing questions, and new ways of answering them. It might even show us that there is much more to be said for Anselm's views than we would have thought possible otherwise.

Preface

At various times I wrote three treatises pertaining to the study of Holy Scripture, all of them in question-and-answer form, with the person asking questions identified as 'Teacher' and the respondent as 'Student'. I did in fact write a fourth treatise in the same form—a very useful work, I believe, for those being introduced to dialectic—which begins with the words *"De grammatico."*[1] But since its subject matter is different from these three, I do not count it as belonging with them.

One of the three is *On Truth*: it considers what truth is, in what things truth is commonly said to be, and what justice is. The second is *On Freedom of Choice*: it considers what freedom of choice is, and whether human beings always have it, as well as how many distinctions there are in freedom of choice depending on whether someone has or lacks rectitude of will—freedom of choice having been given to rational creatures in order that they might preserve rectitude of will. In it I elucidated only the natural power of the will to preserve the rectitude that it received, not how necessary it is that the will be supported by grace. The third asks how the devil sinned by not remaining steadfast[2] in the truth, since God did not give him perseverance, which the devil could not have unless God gave it to him; for if God had given it, the devil would have had it, just as the good angels had it because God gave it to them. Although I did discuss the confirmation of

1. *De grammatico* can mean either "On the grammarian" or "On the grammatical"; since the dialogue is in part devoted to distinguishing the two senses, I have left its title untranslated.

2. Cf. John 8:44: the devil "did not remain steadfast in the truth." "Remained steadfast" (Latin: *stetit*) is literally "stood firm." The translation "remained steadfast" has certain advantages, not the least of which is that it allows the use of 'steadfastness' to translate the cognate noun *status* in *DCD* 6.

1

of the good angels in this treatise, I called it *On the Fall of the Devil* because what I wrote about the bad angels was the very heart of the question, whereas what I said about the good angels was a side issue.

Although I did not compose these treatises one right after the other, their subject matter and their similarity of form require that they be written together as a unit, and in the order in which I have listed them. So even if certain overhasty persons have transcribed them in a different order before they were all finished, I want them to be arranged as I have instructed here.

ON TRUTH

Chapters

Chapter 1

That truth has no beginning or end

STUDENT: Since we believe that God is truth,[1] and we say that truth is in many other things, I would like to know whether, wherever truth is said to be, we must acknowledge that God is that truth. For you yourself, in your *Monologion*, prove on the basis of the truth of speech that the supreme Truth has no beginning or end: "Let anyone who can do so think of this: when did it begin

---

1. Cf. John 14:6, where Christ says, "I am the way, the truth, and the life."

3

to be true, or when was it not true, that something was going to exist? Or when will it cease to be true, and no longer be true, that something existed in the past? But if neither of these can be thought, and neither statement can be true apart from truth, then it is impossible even to think that truth has a beginning or end. Finally, if truth had a beginning or will have an end, before it came into being it was then true that there was no truth, and after it has ceased to exist, it will then be true that there is no truth. Now nothing can be true apart from truth. So truth existed before truth existed, and truth will exist after truth has ceased to exist— which is an absolute absurdity. So, whether truth is said to have a beginning or an end or is understood not to have a beginning or an end, truth cannot be confined by any beginning or end." So you say in your *Monologion*.[2] And for that reason I am eager for you to teach me a definition of truth.

TEACHER: I don't remember ever discovering a definition of truth; but if you like, let's inquire what truth is by examining the variety of things in which we say there is truth.

S: Even if I can't do anything else, I will at least help by listening.

Chapter 2

On the truth of signification, and on the two truths of a statement

T: Then let's inquire first what truth is in a statement, since we quite often call a statement true or false.

S: You inquire, and I will hold on to whatever you discover.

T: When is a statement true?

S: When what it states, whether by affirming or denying, is the case. For I say that it states something even when it denies that what-is-not is, since that is the way in which it states what is the case.

T: So do you think that the thing stated is the truth of the statement?

S: No.

T: Why not?

S: Because nothing is true except by participating in truth, and so the truth of what is true is in the true thing itself, whereas the thing stated is not in the true statement. Hence, we must say that

2. *Monologion* 18.

the thing stated is not the truth of the statement, but the cause of its truth. For this reason it seems to me that the truth of a statement must be sought nowhere else but in the statement itself.

T: Then consider whether the statement itself, or its signification, or any of those things that are in the definition of 'statement', is what you are looking for.

S: I don't think so.

T: Why not?

S: Because if that were so, the statement would always be true, since everything in the definition of 'statement' remains the same, both when what is stated is the case and when it isn't. For the statement is the same, its signification is the same, and so forth.

T: Then what do you think truth is in a statement?

S: All I know is that when a statement signifies that what-is is, then there is truth in it, and it is true.

T: For what purpose is an affirmation made?

S: For signifying that what-is is.

T: So it ought to do that.

S: Certainly.

T: So when it signifies that what-is is, it signifies what it ought to.

S: Obviously.

T: And when it signifies what it ought to, it signifies correctly.

S: Yes.

T: Now when it signifies correctly, its signification is correct.

S: No doubt about it.

T: So when it signifies that what-is is, its signification is correct.

S: That follows.

T: Furthermore, when it signifies that what-is is, its signification is true.

S: Indeed it is both correct and true when it signifies that what-is is.

T: Then its being correct is the same thing as its being true: namely, its signifying that what-is is.

S: Indeed, they are the same.

T: So its truth is nothing other than its rectitude.[3]

---

3. I.e., its correctness. 'Rectitude' (*rectitudo*) is the abstract noun corresponding to 'correct' (*rectum*). I use 'rectitude' rather than 'correctness' for the sake of consistency: later in the dialogue there are passages where 'correctness' will not work as a translation for '*rectitudo*', and since '*rectitudo*' is the most important technical term in the dialogue, it seemed important to signal its presence with a consistent translation.

S: Now I see clearly that this truth[4] is rectitude.

T: The case is similar when a statement signifies that what-is-not is not.

S: I understand what you're saying. But teach me how I could respond if someone were to say that even when a statement signifies that what-is-not is, it signifies what it ought to. A statement, after all, has received the power to signify[5] both that what-is is, and that what-is-not is—for if it had not received the power to signify that even what-is-not is, it would not signify this.[6] So even when it signifies that what-is-not is, it signifies what it ought to. But if, as you have shown, it is correct and true by signifying what it ought to, then a statement is true even when it states that what-is-not is.

T: Certainly it is not customary to call a statement true when it signifies that what-is-not is; nonetheless, it has truth and rectitude, in that it is doing what it ought to. But when it signifies that what-is is, it is doing what it ought to in *two* ways, since it not only signifies what it received the power to signify but also signifies in keeping with the purpose for which it was made. We customarily call a statement true according to the rectitude and truth by which it signifies that what-is is, not according to that by which it signifies that even what-is-not is. After all, what a statement ought to do depends more on the purpose for which it received its power of signification than on what was not the purpose for receiving signification; and the only reason it received the power to signify that a thing is when it is not, or that a thing is not when it is, was that it was not possible for it to be given only the power of signifying that a thing is when it is, or that it is not when it is not.

4. "This truth": i.e., the truth of statements.

5. "Has received the power to signify" is literally just "has received to signify" (*accepit significare*). Anselm uses this construction and others like it in the three dialogues to speak about the powers and capacities that things receive from whatever causes them to exist in the first place.

6. In other words, a false statement is still a meaningful statement: if I say "Abraham Lincoln served out his second term as president," I do manage to signify that Abraham Lincoln served out his second term, even though what I am signifying does not match the way things really are. The student therefore suggests that what statements were made for (what they "received the power to do") is signifying, period, and not necessarily signifying what is really the case.

Therefore, the rectitude and truth that a statement has because it signifies in keeping with the purpose for which it was made is one thing; that which it has because it signifies what it received the power to signify is quite another. The latter is invariable for a given statement, whereas the former is variable, since a statement always has the latter but does not always have the former. For it has the latter naturally, whereas it has the former accidentally and according to its use. For example, when I say "It is day" in order to signify that what-is is, I am using the signification of this statement correctly, since this is the purpose for which it was made; consequently, in that case it is said to signify correctly. But when I use the same statement to signify that what-is-not is, I am not using it correctly, since it was not made for that purpose; and so in that case its signification is said not to be correct. Now in some statements these two rectitudes or truths are inseparable: for example, when we say "Human beings are animals" or "A human being is not a stone." For this affirmation always signifies that what-is is, and this negation always signifies that what-is-not is not; nor can we use the former to signify that what-is-not is (since human beings are always animals) or the latter to signify that what-is is not (since a human being is never a stone).[7]

We began our inquiry with the truth that a statement has when someone uses it correctly, since it is according to this truth that common usage identifies a statement as true. As for the truth that it cannot fail to have, we will discuss that later.[8]

S: Then go back to what you began, since you have adequately distinguished for me between the two truths of statements—if,

---

7. Anselm is noting that statements can be regarded as having two functions and therefore as being true in two different senses. Their real purpose is to signify what is the case, so they can be called true if they signify what is the case (that is the usual sense of 'true'); but they also have the power simply to signify, regardless of whether what they signify is the case, and so they can be called true if they simply signify. Any well-formed statement signifies (so Anselm says that this sort of truth is "invariable" and "natural"), but not every well-formed statement signifies what is the case (so Anselm says that this sort of truth is "variable"). The last two sentences note that there are certain statements in which the two truths cannot diverge: that is, if they signify anything at all, they signify what is the case. These are the affirmations of necessary truths and the negations of necessary falsehoods.

8. There is a brief discussion of this truth at the end of chapter 5.

that is, you have shown that a statement has some truth even when it's a lie, as you say.

T: For the time being, let these remarks suffice for our first topic, the truth of signification. After all, the same notion of truth that we examined in spoken statements will be found in all signs that are made for the purpose of signifying that something is or is not: for example, writing and sign language.

S: Then go on to the other things.

Chapter 3

On the truth of opinion

T: We also call a thought true when things are as we think they are (whether we think this through reason or in some other way) and false when they are not.

S: That's the custom.

T: So what do you think truth in thought is?

S: According to the reasoning we found persuasive in the case of statements, nothing can be more correctly called the truth of a thought than its rectitude. For the power of thinking that something is or is not was given to us in order that we might think that what-is is, and that what-is-not is not. Therefore, if someone thinks that what-is is, he is thinking what he ought to think, and so his thought is correct. If, then, a thought is true and correct for no other reason than that we are thinking that what-is is, or that what-is-not is not, its truth is nothing other than its rectitude.

T: Your reasoning is correct.

Chapter 4

On the truth of the will

Now Truth Itself says that there is also truth in the will when he says that the devil "did not remain steadfast in the truth" [John 8:44]. For it was only in his will that he was in the truth and then abandoned the truth.

S: So I believe. For if he had always willed what he ought, he would never have sinned; and it was only by sinning that he abandoned the truth.

T: Then tell me what you understand truth to be in the will.

S: Nothing other than rectitude. For if he was in rectitude and in the truth so long as he willed what he ought—i.e., that for the

sake of which he had received a will—and if he abandoned rectitude and truth when he willed what he ought not, then we cannot understand truth in this case as anything other than rectitude,
since both truth and rectitude in his will were nothing other than
his willing what he ought.

T: You understand this well.

Chapter 5
On the truth of natural and non-natural action

But we must equally believe that there is truth in action as well.
As the Lord says, "He who does evil hates the light" [John 3:20],
and "He who does the truth comes to the light" [John 3:21].

S: I understand what you're saying.

T: Then consider, if you can, what truth is in action.

S: Unless I am mistaken, we must use the same reasoning
about truth in action that we used earlier to identify truth in other
things.

T: You're right. For if doing evil and doing the truth are oppo-
sites, as the Lord indicates by saying that "He who does evil hates
the light" and "He who does the truth comes to the light," then
doing the truth is the same as doing good, since doing good and
doing evil are contraries. Therefore, if doing the truth and doing
good are both opposed to the same thing, they have the same signification. Now everyone agrees that those who do what they
ought, do good and act correctly.[9] From this it follows that to act
correctly is to do the truth, since it is agreed that to do the truth is
to do good, and to do good is to act correctly. So nothing is more
obvious than that the truth of action is its rectitude.

S: I see no weakness in your reasoning.

T: Consider whether every action that does what it ought to
is appropriately said to do the truth. You see, there is rational
action, such as giving to charity, and irrational action, such as
the action of a fire that causes heat. So think about whether it
would be appropriate for us to say that the fire is doing the
truth.

S: If the fire received the power to heat from the one from
whom it has being, then when it heats, it is doing what it ought
to. So I don't see what is inappropriate about saying that the fire
does the truth and acts correctly when it does what it ought to.

---

9. "Act correctly" is literally "do rectitude."

T: That's exactly how it seems to me. Hence we can note that there is one rectitude or truth in action that is necessary, and another that is not. When the fire heats, it does the truth and acts correctly out of necessity; but when human beings do good, it is not out of necessity that they do the truth and act correctly. Now when the Lord said that "He who does the truth comes to the light," he meant us to take 'do' not just to mean what is properly* called doing, but as substituting for any verb. After all, he is not excluding from this truth or light someone who undergoes persecution "for righteousness' sake" [Matthew 5:10], or who is when and where he ought to be, or who stands or sits when he ought to, and so forth. No one says that such people are not doing good. And when the Apostle[10] says that everyone will receive a recompense "according to his deeds" [2 Corinthians 5:10], we should understand him to mean whatever we customarily identify as doing good or doing evil.

S: Ordinary language, too, uses 'to do' both of undergoing and of many other things that are not doings. Hence, if I am not mistaken, we can also include among right actions an upright will, whose truth we investigated earlier, before the truth of action.

T: You are not mistaken. For someone who wills what he ought to is said to act correctly and to do good; nor is he excluded from those who do the truth. But since we are discussing the upright will in the course of investigating the truth, and the Lord seems to speak specifically of the truth that is in the will when he says that the devil "did not remain steadfast in the truth," I wanted to give separate consideration to what truth is in the will.

S: I am glad you did it that way.

T: So since it is established that there is a natural truth in action as well as a non-natural truth, that truth in statements which we saw above cannot be separated from them should be classified as natural truth.[11] For just as fire, when it heats, does the

10. I.e., the Apostle Paul.

11. See chapter 2. The truth that cannot be separated from a statement is its signifying whatever it "received the power to signify." This truth, Anselm says, is akin to the truth of natural action. Just as fire cannot help heating, "It is day" cannot help signifying that it is day. In this sense, both the statement and the fire are doing what they received the power to do, and so they are both "doing the truth."

truth, since it received the power to heat from the one who gave it being, so also the statement "It is day" does the truth when it signifies that it is day, whether it is actually day or not, since it received naturally the power to do this.

S: Now for the first time I see the truth in a false statement.

Chapter 6

On the truth of the senses

T: Do you think we have found every dwelling-place of truth apart from the supreme Truth?

S: I now recall one truth that I don't find in the things you have discussed.

T: What is it?

S: There is truth in the bodily senses, although not always, since they sometimes deceive us. For sometimes when I see something through glass, my vision deceives me, since it sometimes reports to me that the body* I see beyond the glass is the same color as the glass, when in fact it is a different color; on the other hand, sometimes it makes me think that the glass has the color of the thing that I see beyond it, even though it doesn't. And there are many other cases in which vision and the other senses are deceptive.

T: I don't think this truth and falsehood is in the senses, but in opinion. For it is the interior sense that deceives itself; the exterior sense does not lie to it. Sometimes this is easy to recognize, but sometimes it is difficult. When a child fears the open maw of the sculpture of a dragon, it is easy to recognize that his vision is not responsible; his vision is reporting to the child exactly what it reports to adults. Rather, what is responsible is the child's interior sense, which is not yet adept at distinguishing between a thing and its likeness. This is the sort of thing that happens when we see someone who resembles someone else and we think he is the person he resembles, or when someone hears what is not a human voice and thinks it is a human voice. The interior sense is responsible for these as well.

Now what you say about glass is the case for the following reason. When vision passes through a body* that is of the same color as air—unless that body is denser or darker than the air—nothing prevents vision from taking on the likeness of the color that it sees beyond that body, any more than when it passes through air.

This is what happens when, for example, vision passes through glass with its natural color (i.e., in which there is no admixture of another color) or through perfectly pure water or crystal or something of a similar color. But when vision passes through another color—as, for example, through glass that is not its natural color, but to which some other color has been added—it receives the color that it encounters first. Hence, once it has received a color and been affected by it, any other color it encounters is received either less accurately or not at all; as a result, what it reports is the color it first received, either by itself or in conjunction with a color it encounters afterward. For if vision is altered by a prior color to the full extent of its power to see color, it cannot perceive any other color at the same time; but if it is not altered to the full extent of its power to perceive color, it can perceive another color. For example, if it passes through some body, such as glass, that is so perfectly red that vision itself is completely altered by its redness, it cannot be altered by any other color at the same time. But if it does not find the redness it first encounters to exhaust its power to see color, it is (so to speak) not yet full; it can still take on another color, since its capacity was not satiated by the previous color. Someone who does not know this therefore thinks his vision is reporting that everything it perceives after taking on the first color is either partially or wholly of that same color. And so it happens that the interior sense blames its own shortcoming on the exterior sense.

Similarly, when a straight stick, part of which is in water and part of which is not, is thought to be broken; or when we think we see our own faces in a mirror; or when we think our vision or other senses are reporting that any number of things are otherwise than they really are, it is not the fault of the senses. They are reporting what they can, since that is what they received the power to do. Instead, the blame lies with the judgment of the soul, which does not discriminate well what the senses can or ought to do. To show that this is so would be more troublesome than fruitful for our present purposes, so I don't think we should take up this topic just now. Let it suffice to say that whatever the senses seem to report, whether they do so by their very nature or in virtue of some other cause, they are doing what they ought to. Hence they are acting correctly and doing the truth, and this truth is included in the truth of action.

S: I am happy with your reply, and I don't want you to spend any more time on this question about the senses.

Chapter 7
On the truth of the being[12] of things

T: Now consider whether, apart from the supreme Truth, we should understand truth to exist in any thing besides those we examined above.

S: What could that be?

T: Do you think anything is,[13] in any time or place, that is not in the supreme Truth and did not receive its being, insofar as it has being, from the supreme Truth, or that can be anything other than what it is in the supreme Truth?

S: That is unthinkable.

T: So whatever is, truly is, insofar as it is what it is in the supreme Truth.

S: You can conclude without reservation that everything that is, truly is, since it is nothing other than what it is in the supreme Truth.

T: So there is a truth in the being of all things that are, since they are what they are in the supreme Truth.

S: I recognize that there is truth in their being in such a way that there can be no falsehood there, since whatever is falsely, is not.

T: Well said! But tell me whether anything ought to be different from what it is in the supreme Truth.

S: No.

T: Therefore, if all things are what they are in the supreme Truth, they are undoubtedly what they ought to be.

S: Indeed they are.

T: Now whatever is what it ought to be, is correct.[14]

S: It could not be otherwise.

T: So everything that is, is correct.

S: Nothing could be more logical.

---

12. See essence* (4).

13. As often in these dialogues, 'is' includes the meanings 'exists', 'is a certain way', and 'is the case'.

14. Literally, "is correctly." I could say "exists correctly," but the context makes clear that Anselm is not using the verb *'esse'* ("to be") solely to denote existence. Something can be what it ought to be, not merely by existing, but by being in the place it ought to be, having the characteristics it ought to have, and so on.

T: So if both truth and rectitude are in the being of things because they are what they are in the supreme Truth, it is clear that the truth of things is their rectitude.

S: Nothing could be plainer than the soundness of your argument.

Chapter 8

On the various meanings of 'ought' and 'ought not', 'can' and 'cannot'

But how can we say, with respect to the truth of a thing, that whatever is ought to be, since there are many evil deeds that certainly ought not to be?

T: How is it surprising that the same thing both ought to be and ought not to be?

S: How can that be the case?

T: I know you do not doubt that nothing is at all, unless God either causes or permits it.

S: There is nothing I am more certain of.

T: Will you dare to say that God causes or permits anything unwisely or badly?

S: On the contrary, I contend that God always acts wisely and well.

T: Do you think that something caused or permitted by such great goodness and wisdom ought not to be?

S: What intelligent person would dare to think that?

T: Therefore, both what comes about because God causes it and what comes about because God permits it ought equally to be.

S: What you are saying is obviously true.

T: Then tell me whether you think the effect of an evil will ought to be.

S: That's the same as asking whether an evil deed ought to be, and no sensible person would concede that.

T: And yet God permits some people to perform the evil deeds that their evil wills choose.

S: If only he did not permit it so often!

T: Then the same thing both ought to be and ought not to be. It ought to be, in that God, without whose permission it could not come about, acts wisely and well in permitting it; but if we consider the one whose evil will instigates the action, it ought not to be. In this way the Lord Jesus, who alone was innocent, ought not to have suffered death, and no one ought to have inflicted death on him; and yet he ought to have suffered death, in that he himself wisely and generously and usefully willed to suffer it. There are, after all, many ways in which one and the same thing takes on contrary attributes when considered in different ways. This often happens in the case of an action: for example, punishment.[15] Punishment involves both an agent and a patient, so it can be called both an action and a passion.[16] Even though 'action' and 'punishment' and similar words that are derived from passive participles are used with an active signification, they seem to belong more to the patient than to the agent. In referring to that which acts, it would seem more appropriate to speak of 'acting' or 'punishing', and to use 'action' and 'punishment' in speaking of that which undergoes the action. For 'acting' and 'punishing' get their name from the one who acts and punishes, as foresight gets its name from the one who foresees and restraint from the one who restrains—and those who act, punish, foresee, and restrain are active; by contrast, 'action' and 'punishment' are derived from those who are acted upon and punished, and they are passive.[17] But since—to give you one example from which you will understand the rest—just as there is not someone who pun-

15. Anselm actually speaks of a blow (*percussio*). But the argument that follows, if it is to be rendered into English intelligibly, requires a noun with a cognate verb; that verb in turn must have a participle that is distinct in form from the noun. (The latter requirement rules out 'striking' and 'beating', which appear in other translations.) 'Punishment', with 'punish' and 'punishing' available, fits the bill, and is close enough in sense to *percussio* to allow me to keep intact the example Anselm uses in the last paragraph of this speech.

16. 'Patient' and 'passion' are technical terminology. A patient is someone who is on the receiving end of an action, as opposed to the agent, who performs the action. A passion is an undergoing, as opposed to an action, which is a doing. If A punishes B, A is the agent and B the patient; A's punishing B is an action, and B's being punished by A is a passion.

17. Literally: "For [the nouns] 'acting' and 'striking' get their name from [the present participles] 'acting' and 'striking', as [the noun] 'foresight' gets its name from [the present participle] 'foreseeing' and [the noun] 'restraint' from [the present participle] 'restraining'—and [the participles] 'acting', 'striking', 'foreseeing', and 'restraining' are active; by contrast, [the nouns] 'action' (*actio*) and 'blow' (*percussio*) are derived from [the participles] *actum* and *percussum*, which are passive."

ishes unless there is also someone who is punished, nor someone punished without someone who punishes, so punishing and punishment cannot exist without each other. Indeed, they are one and the same thing under different names, depending on the different roles being signified. That's why punishment is said to belong to both the one who punishes and the one who is punished.

Hence, one and the same action will be evaluated in the same or in opposite ways for the agent and the patient, according to whether the agent and patient themselves are evaluated in the same or in opposite ways. Therefore, when the one who punishes punishes correctly, and the one who is punished is punished correctly—as when a sinner is corrected by one with the authority to correct him—the action is correct on both sides, since on both sides there ought to be punishment. By contrast, when a just man is punished by a wicked man, since the just man ought not to be punished and the wicked man ought not to punish, the action is not correct on either side, since there ought not to be punishment on either side. But when a sinner is punished by someone who lacks the authority to punish him, it cannot be denied that the punishment is both correct and not correct, since it both ought to be and ought not to be: for the sinner ought to be punished, but this man ought not to punish him. But if you look to the judgment of the supreme Wisdom and Goodness and ask whether the punishment ought not to be (whether on one side only or on the part of both agent and patient), who would dare to deny that what is permitted by such great Wisdom and Goodness ought to be?

S: Let him deny it who dares; I certainly do not dare.

T: And what if you are thinking in terms of the nature of things: would you say that when iron nails were driven into the Lord's body, his feeble flesh ought not to have been pierced, or that, once pierced by the sharp iron, he ought not to have suffered pain?

S: I would be speaking against nature.

T: So it can happen that according to nature an action or passion ought to be, while with respect to the agent or patient it ought not to be, since the agent ought not to do it and the patient ought not to undergo it.

S: I can't deny any of that.

T: Do you see, then, that it can happen quite often that the same action both ought to be and ought not to be, when considered in different ways?

S: You are showing this so clearly that I cannot fail to see it.

T: Now one thing I want you to know is that 'ought' and 'ought not' are sometimes used improperly:* for example, if I say that I ought to be loved by you. For if it's true that I ought to be loved by you, then I am under an obligation to do what I ought,[18] and I am at fault if I am not loved by you.

S: That follows.

T: But when I ought to be loved by you, the love is not to be demanded from me, but from you.

S: I must admit that's true.

T: So when I say that I ought to be loved by you, it does not mean that there is something I ought to do, but that you ought to love me. Similarly, when I say that I ought not to be loved by you, this is understood to mean simply that you ought not to love me. We talk about abilities and inabilities in the same way: for example, if someone says that Hector was able to be defeated by Achilles, and Achilles was not able to be defeated by Hector. After all, the ability was not in the one who was able to be defeated, but in the one who was able to defeat him; nor was the inability in the one who could not be defeated, but in the one who could not defeat him.

S: I like what you're saying. In fact, I think it is useful to understand this.

T: You're right to think so.

Chapter 9

That every action signifies something true or false

But let's return to the truth of signification, which I began with in order to lead you from the better-known to the less well-known. For everyone talks about the truth of signification, but few consider the truth that is in the being of things.

S: Your leading me in that order has been a great help to me.

T: Then let us see how widespread the truth of signification is. For there is true and false signification not only in what we usually call signs, but also in all the other things we have discussed. After all, since no one should do anything but what he ought to do, by the very fact that someone does something, he

---

18. Literally, "I am one who is indebted to pay back what I owe": the Latin plays on the fact that *debere* means both 'owe' and 'ought', and that the noun *debitor* (debtor, one who is indebted) can mean 'one who has an obligation'.

says and signifies that he ought to do it. And if he ought to do what he does, he says something true; but if he ought not, he lies.

S: I think I understand, but since I have never heard this before, explain more clearly what you mean.

T: Suppose you were in a place where you knew there were both healthful and deadly herbs, but you didn't know how to tell them apart. And suppose someone were there who you did not doubt knew how to tell them apart, and when you asked him which were healthful and which deadly, he said that certain ones were healthful but then ate others. Which would you believe more: his words or his action?

S: I would believe his action more than his words.

T: Then he would have told you which were healthful by his action more than by his words.

S: That's true.

T: Similarly, if you didn't know that one ought not to lie, and someone lied in your presence, then even if he told you that he ought not to lie, he would tell you by his action that he ought to lie more than he would tell you by his words that he ought not. Likewise, when someone thinks or wills something, if you didn't know whether he ought to think or will it, then if you could see his will and thought, he would signify to you by that very action that he ought to think and will it. Now if he in fact ought to think or will it, he would be saying something true; but if not, he would be lying. And similarly, there is also true and false signification in the being of things, since by the very fact that something is, it says that it ought to be.

S: Now I see clearly what I had never realized before.

T: Let's go on to what remains.

S: You lead, and I'll follow.

Chapter 10

On the supreme Truth

T: You will surely not deny that the supreme Truth is rectitude.

S: Indeed, I cannot acknowledge it to be anything else.

T: Note that, while all the rectitudes discussed earlier are rectitudes because the things in which they exist either are or do what they ought, the supreme Truth is not a rectitude because it ought to be or do anything. For all things are under obligations to it, but it is under no obligation to anything.[19] Nor is there any reason why it is what it is, except that it is.

S: I understand.

T: Do you also see that this rectitude is the cause of all other truths and rectitudes, and nothing is the cause of it?

S: I see that, and I notice that some of these other truths and rectitudes are merely effects, whereas others are both causes and effects. For example, the truth that is in the being of things is an effect of the supreme Truth, and it is in turn a cause of the truth of thoughts and statements; and the latter two truths are not a cause of any other truth.

T: You have understood this well. Hence, you can now understand how I used the truth of statements in my *Monologion* to prove that the supreme Truth has no beginning or end. For when I asked, "When was it not true that something was going to exist?"[20] I didn't mean that this statement, asserting that something was going to exist in the future, was itself without a beginning, or that this truth was God. Instead I meant that it is inconceivable that this statement could ever have been uttered without its also possessing truth. Therefore, since it is inconceivable that that truth could fail to exist if the statement existed in which that truth could exist, we understand that the Truth that is the first cause of this truth existed without a beginning. After all, the truth of a statement could not always exist if its cause did not always exist. For a statement that says something will exist in the future is not true unless in fact something will exist in the future; and nothing will exist in the future unless it exists in the supreme Truth. The same reasoning applies to a statement that says something existed in the past. Since it is inconceivable that this statement, if uttered, could lack truth, it must be the case that the supreme cause of its truth cannot be understood to have an end. For what makes it true to say that something existed in the past is the fact that something really did exist in the past; and the reason something existed in the past is that this is how things are in the supreme Truth. Therefore, if it was never possible for it not to be true that something was going to exist, and it will never be possi-

---

19. More literally, ". . . the supreme Truth is not a rectitude because it owes something. For all things owe [something] to it, but it owes nothing to anything." Recall that 'ought' and 'owe' are the same word in Latin.

20. *Monologion* 18, as quoted at the beginning of the dialogue.

ble for it not to be true that something existed in the past, it is impossible for the supreme Truth ever to have had a beginning or ever to have an end.

S: I see no way to object to your reasoning.

Chapter 11
On the definition of truth

T: Let's return to the investigation of truth that we have begun.

S: All of this is relevant to investigating truth, but return to what you wish.

T: Then tell me whether you think there is any other rectitude besides those we have discussed.

S: I don't think there is any, except that which is in corporeal things, which is very different from those we have discussed— for example, the rectitude[21] of a stick.

T: In what way do you think this differs from those?

S: In that this can be known through corporeal vision, whereas the others are perceived by reason.

T: Can't that rectitude of bodies* be understood and known through reason apart from the subject?[22] If, when a body is not present, you are in doubt whether its surface is straight, and it can be shown that it is not curved in any place, are you not grasping by reason that it must be straight?

S: Certainly. But this same rectitude that is understood by reason in this way is also perceived by vision in the subject. The others, however, can be perceived only by the mind.

T: Then if I'm not mistaken, we can define truth as rectitude perceptible only by the mind.

S: I don't see any way that someone saying that could be mistaken. For this definition of truth contains neither more nor less than it should, since the term 'rectitude' distinguishes truth from everything that is not called rectitude, and the phrase 'perceptible only by the mind' distinguishes it from visible rectitude.

---

21. I.e., straightness.

22. "The subject": the physical object that has the property in question (in this case, straightness).

Chapter 12
On the definition of justice

But since you have taught me that all truth is rectitude, and rectitude seems to me to be the same thing as justice, teach me also what I should understand justice to be. It seems, after all, that if it is right for something to be,[23] it is also just for it to be; and conversely, if it is just for something to be, it is also right for it to be. For it seems to be both just and right for fire to be hot and for all human beings to love those who love them. Indeed, if—as I believe—whatever ought to be is right and just, and nothing is right and just but what ought to be, then justice cannot be anything other than rectitude. Certainly justice and rectitude are the same in the supreme and simple* nature, although he is not just and right because he is under any obligation.

T: So if justice is nothing other than rectitude, you have your definition of justice. And since we are speaking of the rectitude that is perceptible only by the mind, truth and rectitude and justice are all interdefined, so that someone who knows one and not the others can attain knowledge of those he doesn't know through the one he does know. Or rather, someone who knows one cannot fail to know the others.

S: What then? Shall we say that a stone is just when it seeks to go from higher to lower, since it is doing what it ought to, in the same way that we say human beings are just when they do what they ought to?

T: We don't generally call something 'just' on the basis of that sort of justice.

S: Then why is a human being any more just than a stone is, if both act justly?

T: Don't you think what the human being does differs in some way from what the stone does?

S: I know that the human being acts spontaneously,[24] whereas the stone acts naturally* and not spontaneously.

T: That is why the stone is not called just: something that does what it ought to is not just unless it wills what it does.

---

23. Here again, 'to be' includes the meanings 'to exist', 'to be a certain way', and 'to be the case'.

24. 'Spontaneously' is used as a technical term in this translation; the word does not have the connotations it has in ordinary usage. For a definition, see the Glossary.

S: Then shall we say that a horse is just when it wills to graze, since it willingly does what it ought to?

T: I did not say that something is just if it willingly does what it ought to, but that something is not just if it does not willingly do what it ought to.

S: Then tell me who is just.

T: I see that you are looking for a definition of the justice that deserves praise, just as its opposite, injustice, deserves reproach.

S: That's what I'm looking for.

T: Clearly that justice is not in any nature that is not aware of rectitude. For whatever does not will rectitude, even if it in fact retains rectitude, does not deserve praise for retaining it; and what does not know rectitude cannot will it.

S: That's true.

T: So the rectitude that wins praise for the one who retains it exists only in a rational nature, since only a rational nature perceives the rectitude of which we are speaking.

S: That follows.

T: Therefore, since all justice is rectitude, the justice that makes praiseworthy the one who preserves it does not exist anywhere at all except in rational natures.

S: That must be right.

T: Where, then, do you think this justice exists in human beings, who are rational?

S: Either in the will, or in knowledge, or in action.

T: If someone understands correctly or acts correctly, but does not will correctly, will anyone praise him for his justice?

S: No.

T: Therefore, this justice is not rectitude of knowledge or rectitude of action, but rectitude of will.

S: It is either that or nothing.

T: Do you think we have reached an adequate definition of the justice we're investigating?

S: You had better say.

T: Do you think everyone who wills what he ought to wills correctly and has rectitude of will?

S: If someone unknowingly wills what he ought to—for example, if someone wills to lock the door against one who, unbeknownst to him, intends to kill someone in the house—then whether or not he has *some* rectitude of will, he doesn't have the rectitude of will we're asking about.

T: What do you say about someone who knows that he ought to will what he wills?

S: It can turn out that someone who knowingly wills what he ought to is also unwilling to be under that obligation. For example, if a robber is forced to give back the money he stole, he clearly does not will to be under that obligation, since he is forced to will to give it back because he ought to. But in no way does he deserve praise for this rectitude.

T: Someone who gives food to a starving pauper for the sake of an empty reputation[25] wills that he be under the obligation to will what he in fact wills. For he is praised because he wills to do what he ought to. What do you think about him?

S: His rectitude does not deserve praise, and so it is not sufficient for the justice we're asking about. But show me now what *is* sufficient.

T: Every will not only wills something but also wills for the sake of something. Now just as we must examine what it wills, so also we must understand why it wills. In fact, a will should not be correct because it wills what it ought to will more than because it wills it for the reason it ought to will. Hence, every will has a what and a why. For we do not will anything at all unless there is a reason why we will it.

S: We all recognize this in ourselves.

T: But what do you think is the *why* on account of which everyone must will whatever he wills, if he is to have a praiseworthy will? *What* everyone must will is clear, after all, since someone who does not will what he ought to is not just.

S: It seems no less obvious to me that just as everyone must will *what* he ought, so also everyone must will it *because* he ought, in order for his will to be just.

T: You correctly grasp that these two things are necessary for the will to have justice: to will what it ought to, and because it ought to. But are they sufficient?

S: Why wouldn't they be?

---

25. "For the sake of an empty reputation": *propter vanam gloriam.* Someone who gives food *propter vanam gloriam* does so in order to win praise for his generosity when in fact he is not generous but self-seeking. Anselm says that such a person "wills to be under an obligation to will what he in fact wills" because if he were under no such obligation, he could not win praise for doing as he ought to do. Since he clearly wills the praise, he must also will the obligation.

T: Suppose someone wills what he ought because he is compelled, and he is compelled because he ought to will it. Doesn't
he in a certain sense will what he ought to, because he ought
to?

S: I cannot deny it. But he wills it in one way, and the just man
in quite another.

T: Distinguish these two ways.

S: When the just man wills what he ought, he does not—insofar as he deserves to be called just—preserve rectitude for the
sake of anything other than rectitude itself. But someone who
wills what he ought only because he is compelled, or because he
is bribed by some extraneous reward, preserves rectitude not for
its own sake, but for the sake of something else—if he should be
said to preserve rectitude at all.

T: Then a will is just when it preserves its rectitude for the sake
of that rectitude itself.

S: Either such a will is just, or no will is.

T: Then justice is rectitude of will preserved for its own sake.

S: That is indeed the definition of justice for which I was looking.

T: Now consider whether perhaps something in it needs cor-
recting.

S: I see nothing in it that needs to be corrected.

T: Neither do I, since there is no justice that is not rectitude,
and no rectitude other than rectitude of will is called justice in its
own right. For rectitude of action is called justice, but only when
the action proceeds from a correct will. Rectitude of will, on the
other hand, is always entitled to be called justice, even if it is impossible for what we correctly will to come about.

Now the use of the word 'preserved' might prompt someone to
say that if rectitude of will is to be called justice only when it is
preserved, then it is not justice as soon as we have it, and we do
not receive justice when we receive rectitude of will; rather, we
cause it to be justice by preserving it. After all, we receive and
have rectitude of will before we preserve it. For we do not receive or initially have it because preserve it; instead, we begin
to preserve it because we have received it and have it.

But in response we can say that we simultaneously receive both
the willing and the having of rectitude. For we have it only in
virtue of willing it; and if we will it, we thereby have it. Now just
as we simultaneously have it and will it, so also we simultaneously will it and preserve it. For just as we do not preserve it except when we will it, so also there is no time at which we will it

but do not preserve it; on the contrary, as long as we will it, we preserve it, and as long as we preserve it, we will it. Therefore, since we both will it and have it at the same time, we both will it and preserve it at the same time. Necessarily, we simultaneously receive both the having and the preserving of rectitude. And just as we have it as long as we preserve it, so also we preserve it as long as we have it. Nor does any absurdity follow from these statements. Indeed, just as the receiving of this rectitude is prior* in nature to having or willing it (since neither having nor willing it is the cause of receiving it, but receiving it is the cause of willing and having it) and yet receiving it is temporally simultaneous with having and willing it (since we simultaneously begin to receive it, to have it, and to will it, and no sooner do we receive it than we have it and will it), so also having or willing it, although prior in nature to preserving it, is nonetheless temporally simultaneous with preserving it. Hence, the one from whom we simultaneously receive the having, the willing, and the preserving of rectitude of will is also the one from whom we receive justice; and as soon as we have and will that rectitude of will, it is rightly called "justice."

Now the last phrase we added, 'for its own sake', is so essential that rectitude is in no way justice unless it is preserved for its own sake.

S: I can't think of any objection.

T: Do you think this definition can be applied to the supreme Justice—insofar as we can talk about a thing about which nothing, or hardly anything, can be said properly?*

S: Although in him will and rectitude are not distinct, still, just as we speak of the power of divinity or the divine power or powerful divinity even though in the divinity power is nothing other than divinity, so also it is appropriate for us to speak of God's rectitude of will or voluntary rectitude or upright will. And we cannot so fittingly say of any other rectitude as we can of his that it is preserved for its own sake. For just as nothing else preserves that rectitude but itself, and it preserves itself *through* nothing else but itself, so also it preserves itself *for the sake of* nothing but itself.

T: Then we can unhesitatingly say that justice is rectitude of will that is preserved for its own sake. And since we have no present passive participle of the verb 'preserve', we can use the perfect passive participle of the same verb in place of the present.[26]

S: It is extremely common for us to use perfect passive participles in place of the present passive participles that Latin doesn't have. Similarly, Latin has no perfect participles for active and neuter[27] verbs, so in place of the perfect participles that it doesn't have, it uses present participles. For example, I might say of someone, "that which he learned studying and reading, he doesn't teach unless forced." That is, "what he learned when he studied and read, he does not teach unless he is forced."[28]

T: Then we were right to say that justice is rectitude of will preserved for its own sake—that is, rectitude of will that is being preserved for its own sake. This is why the just are sometimes called "upright in heart," that is, upright in will, and sometimes simply "upright" without the addition of "in heart," since no one else is understood to be upright but those who have an upright will: for example, "Rejoice, all you upright in heart" [Psalm 32:11] and "The upright will see and be glad" [Psalm 107:42].

S: You have made the definition of justice clear enough even for children. Let's pass on to other things.

26. English, however, is better equipped with participles; the present passive participle is 'being preserved'. Anselm's point is best explained as follows: because of the lack of a present passive participle in Latin, the phrase "rectitude of will preserved for its own sake" is ambiguous. It can mean either "rectitude of will that is being preserved for its own sake" or "rectitude of will that has been (or was) preserved for its own sake." In his definition of justice, Anselm means us to understand the phrase in the first way.

27. By 'neuter' verbs Anselm seems to mean intransitive verbs that are active in form. 'Study' (*studere*) is an example of a neuter verb and 'read' (*legere*) of an active verb.

28. The differences between English and Latin grammar again make Anselm's point obscure. In his sample sentence, 'studying' and 'reading' are both present participles, whereas 'forced' is a past ("perfect") participle. His point is that, since the studying and the reading were in the past, whereas the being-forced is in the present, it would be more accurate to use the perfect participles of 'study' and 'read' and the present participle of 'force' rather than vice versa—the only problem being that Latin does not *have* those participles. Once again, English is better supplied: the relevant participles are 'having studied', 'having read', and 'being forced'.

Chapter 13
That there is one truth in all true things

T: Let's return to rectitude or, in other words, truth—since we are speaking of rectitude perceptible only by the mind, these two words, 'rectitude' and 'truth', signify one thing, which is the genus* of justice—and ask whether there is only one truth in all the things in which we say there is truth, or whether there are several* truths, just as there are several things in which (as we have established) there is truth.

S: I very much want to know that.

T: It has been established that in whatever thing there is truth, that truth is nothing other than rectitude.

S: I don't doubt it.

T: So if there are several truths corresponding to the several things in which there is truth, there are also several rectitudes.

S: That is no less certain.

T: If there must be diverse rectitudes corresponding to the diversities of things, then these rectitudes have their being in virtue of the things themselves; and as the things in which they exist change, the rectitudes must also change.

S: Show me one example involving something in which we say there is rectitude, so that I can understand it in others as well.

T: I am saying that if the rectitude of signification differs from rectitude of will because the one is in the will and the other in signification, then rectitude of signification has its being because of signification and varies according to signification.

S: So it does. For when a statement signifies that what-is is, or that what-is-not is not, the signification is correct; and it has been established that this is the rectitude without which there is no correct signification. If, however, the statement signifies that what-is-not is, or that what-is is not, or if it signifies nothing at all, there will be no rectitude of signification, which exists only in signification. Hence, the rectitude of signification has its being through signification and changes along with it, just as color has its being and nonbeing through body.* For when a body exists, its color must exist; and if the body ceases to exist, its color cannot remain.

T: Color is not related to body in the same way that rectitude is related to signification.

S: Explain the difference.

T: If no one wills to signify by any sign what ought to be signified, will there be any signification by means of signs?

S: No.

T: And will it therefore not be right for what-ought-to-be-signified to be signified?

S: It will not be any less right, nor will rectitude demand it any less.

T: Therefore, even when signification doesn't exist, the rectitude in virtue of which it is right for what-ought-to-be-signified to be signified, and by which this is demanded, does not cease to exist.

S: If that rectitude ceased to exist, this would not be right, and rectitude would not demand it.

T: Do you think that when what-ought-to-be-signified is signified, the signification is correct on account of and in accordance with this very rectitude?

S: Indeed, I cannot think otherwise. For if the signification is correct through some other rectitude, there is nothing to keep it from being correct even if this rectitude ceases to exist. But in fact there is no correct signification that signifies what it is not right to signify, or what rectitude does not demand.

T: Then no signification is correct through any rectitude other than that which remains even when signification ceases.

S: That's clear.

T: So when rectitude is present in signification, it's not because rectitude begins to exist in signification when someone signifies that what-is is, or that what-is-not is not; instead, it's because at that time signification comes about in accordance with a rectitude that always exists. And when rectitude is absent from signification, it's not because rectitude ceases to exist when signification is not what it should be or there is no signification at all; instead, it's because at that time signification falls away from a rectitude that never fails. Don't you see that?

S: I see it so clearly that I cannot fail to see it.

T: Therefore, the rectitude by which signification is called correct does not have its being or any change because of signification, no matter how signification itself might change.

S: Nothing is clearer to me now.

T: Can you prove that color is related to body in the same way that rectitude is related to signification?

S: I am more apt now to prove that they are very dissimilar.

T: I think you now realize what the proper view is about the will and its rectitude, and about the other things that ought to have rectitude.

S: I fully understand that this very argument proves that however those other things may be, rectitude itself remains unchangeable.

T: Then what do you think follows concerning those rectitudes? Do they differ from one another, or is there one and the same rectitude for all things?

S: I admitted earlier that if there are several* rectitudes because there are several things in which they are observed, they must exist and change in accordance with those things; and it has been demonstrated that this does not happen at all. So it is not the case that there are several rectitudes because there are several things in which they exist.

T: Do you have any other reason for thinking that there are several rectitudes, other than the fact that there are several things in which they exist?

S: Not only do I realize that that's no reason, I also see that no other reason can be found.

T: Then there is one and the same rectitude for all things.

S: So I must acknowledge.

T: Furthermore, if there is rectitude in the things that ought to have it only because they are as they ought to be, and if this is precisely what it is for them to be correct, then it is evident that there is only this one rectitude for all of them.

S: Undeniably.

T: Therefore, there is one truth in all of them.

S: That, too, is undeniable. But explain this: why do we speak of the truth *of* this or that particular thing as if we were distinguishing different truths, when in fact there aren't different truths for different things? Many people will hardly grant that there is no difference between the truth of the will and what is called the truth of action, or of one of the others.

T: Truth is said improperly* to be *of* this or that thing, since truth does not have its being in or from or through the things in which it is said to be. But when things themselves are[29] in accordance with truth, which is always present to those things that are as they ought to be, we speak of the truth of this or that thing—for example, the truth of the will or of action—in the same way in which we speak of the time of this or that thing despite the fact that there is one and the same time for all things that are tempo-

---

29. Again, 'are' includes the meanings 'exist', 'are a certain way', and 'are the case'.

rally simultaneous, and that if this or that thing did not exist, there would still be time. For we do not speak of the time of this or that thing because time is in the things, but because they are in time. And just as time regarded in itself is not called the time of some particular thing, but we speak of the time of this or that thing when we consider the things that are in time, so also the supreme Truth as it subsists in itself is not the truth of some particular thing, but when something is in accordance with it, then it is called the truth or rectitude of that thing.

ON FREEDOM OF CHOICE

Chapters

Chapter 1

That the power to sin does not belong to freedom of choice

STUDENT: Since free choice seems to be incompatible with the grace, predestination, and foreknowledge of God, I want to know what this freedom of choice is, and whether we always have it. For if freedom of choice is "the ability to sin and not to sin," as some are accustomed to say, and we always have that ability, then how is it that we ever need grace? On the other hand, if we do not always have it, why is sin imputed* to us when we sin without free choice?

TEACHER: I don't think freedom of choice is the power to sin and not to sin. After all, if this were its definition, then neither God nor the angels, who cannot sin, would have free choice—which it is impious to say.

S: Why not say that the free choice of God and the good angels is one thing, and our free choice is quite another?

T: Even though human free choice differs from that of God and the good angels, the definition of the word 'freedom' should still be the same for both. For example, even though one animal differs from another, whether substantially* or accidentally,* the definition of the word 'animal' is the same for all animals. Therefore, we ought to offer a definition of freedom of choice that contains neither more nor less than freedom; and since the free choice of God and the good angels cannot sin, "the ability to sin" does not belong in the definition of freedom of choice.

And finally, the power to sin is neither freedom nor a part of freedom—to understand this clearly, pay close attention to what I am about to say.

S: That's why I'm here.

T: Which will do you think is freer: one whose willing and whose ability not to sin are such that it cannot be turned away from the rectitude of not sinning, or one that in some way can be turned to sin?

S: I don't see why a will isn't freer when it is capable of both.

T: Do you not see that someone who has what is fitting and expedient in such a way that he cannot lose it is freer than someone who has it in such a way that he can lose it and be seduced into what is unfitting and inexpedient?

S: I don't think anyone would doubt that.

T: And you will say that it is no less indubitable that sinning is always unfitting and harmful.

S: No one in his right mind thinks otherwise.

T: Then a will that cannot fall away from the rectitude of not sinning is freer than a will that can abandon that rectitude.

S: I don't think anything could be more reasonably asserted.

T: Now if something diminishes freedom if it is added and increases freedom if taken away, do you think that it is either freedom or a part of freedom?

S: I cannot think so.

T: Then the power to sin, which if added to the will diminishes its freedom and if taken away increases it, is neither freedom nor a part of freedom.

S: Nothing could be more logical.

Chapter 2

That nonetheless, angels and human beings sinned through this power and through free choice; and although they were able to be slaves to sin, sin was not able to master them

T: So what is extraneous to freedom in this way does not belong to freedom of choice.

S: I cannot rebut your arguments at all, but it strikes me quite forcefully that in the beginning both the angelic nature and our own had the power to sin—if they had not had it, they would not have sinned. But if both human beings and angels sinned through this power, which is extraneous in this way to free choice, how can we say they sinned through free choice? And if they did not sin through free choice, it seems they sinned out of necessity. After all, they sinned either spontaneously* or out of necessity. And if they sinned spontaneously, how was it not through free choice? So if it was *not* through free choice, they apparently sinned out of necessity.

And there is something else that worries me about this power to sin. Someone who has the power to sin can be a slave to sin, since "he who commits sin is a slave to sin" [John 8:34]. But someone who can be a slave to sin can be mastered by sin. In what way, then, was that nature created free, and what sort of free choice did it have, given that it could be mastered by sin?

T: It was through the power of sinning, and spontaneously, and through free choice, and not out of necessity that our nature,* and

that of the angels, first sinned and were able to be slaves to sin;
and yet sin was not able to master them in such a way that either
they or their choice could be said not to be free.

S: I need you to explain that, because it's obscure to me.

T: The fallen angel and the first human being sinned through
free choice, since they sinned through their own choice, which
was so free that it could not be compelled to sin by any other
thing. And so they are justly reproached, since, having this freedom of choice, they sinned: not because any other thing compelled them, and not out of any necessity, but spontaneously.
They sinned through their choice, which was free; but they did
not sin through that in virtue of which it was free, that is, through
the power by which it was able not to sin and not to be a slave to
sin. Instead, they sinned through that power they had for sinning;
by that power they were neither helped into the freedom not to
sin nor coerced into slavery to sin.

Now as for what you thought was the implication of their
being able to be slaves to sin—namely, that sin was able to
master them, and so neither they nor their choice was free—
that doesn't follow. For if someone has the power not to be a
slave, and no one else has the power to make him a slave, although he can be a slave through his own power, then as long
as he exercises his power not to be a slave rather than his
power to be a slave, nothing can master him and make him a
slave. Suppose a free rich man can make himself the slave of a
poor man. As long as he does not do so, he is still entitled to be
called 'free', and we don't say that the poor man is able to master him—or if we do say this, we say it improperly,* since it is
not in the poor man's power to make him a slave, but in someone else's power.[1] Therefore, nothing prevents it from being the
case that angels and human beings before their sin were free or
had free choice.

Chapter 3

*In what way they had free choice after they had made
themselves slaves to sin, and what free choice is*

S: You have convinced me that of course nothing prevents this
before their sin, but how could they retain free choice after they
had made themselves slaves to sin?

1. The "someone else" is, of course, the rich man himself.

T: Even though they had subjected themselves to sin, they could not destroy the natural freedom of choice within themselves. What they could do, however, was to make themselves unable to exercise that freedom without some additional grace that they had not had before.

S: I believe this, but I want to understand it.

T: Let's first examine what sort of freedom of choice they had before their sin, since it is quite certain that they did in fact have free choice.

S: I'm eager to do so.

T: For what purpose do you think they had this freedom of choice: in order to attain what they willed, or in order to will what they ought to and what was expedient for them to will?

S: In order to will what they ought to and what was expedient to will.

T: So they had freedom of choice for the sake of rectitude of will—since as long as they willed what they ought to, they had rectitude of will.

S: Yes.

T: When we say that they had freedom for the sake of rectitude of will, some ambiguity remains unless we add something. So I ask you this: in what way did they have that freedom for the sake of rectitude of will? Was it in order to attain rectitude without a giver when they did not yet have it; or to receive a rectitude they did not yet have, if it were given to them later so that they might have it; or to abandon the rectitude they had received and then, by their own power, to reclaim what they had abandoned; or to preserve always the rectitude they had received?

S: I do not think they had freedom in order to attain rectitude without a giver, since they were not able to have anything that they did not receive.[2] And we must not say that they had freedom in order to receive from a giver a rectitude they did not yet have, so that they *would* then have it, since we must not believe that they were created without an upright will. Still, we should not deny that they had the freedom to receive that same rectitude if they abandoned it and then were given it back by the one who first gave it to them. We often see this in human beings who by heavenly grace are brought back to righteousness from unrighteousness.

2. Cf. 1 Corinthians 4:7: "What do you have that you did not receive?" See also *DCD* 1.

T: You're right that they were able to receive that lost rectitude if they were given it back; but we are asking about the freedom they had before they sinned—since undoubtedly they had free choice—not about a freedom that none of them would need if they never abandoned the truth.

S: Then I'll go on and reply to the other possibilities you asked about. It's not true that they had freedom in order to abandon rectitude, since to abandon rectitude of will is to sin, and you showed earlier[3] that the power to sin is neither freedom nor a part of freedom. And they didn't receive freedom in order to reclaim, by their own power, the rectitude they had abandoned, since this rectitude was given to them in order that they might never abandon it—for indeed, this very power to reclaim the rectitude they had abandoned would engender carelessness about preserving the rectitude they had. The only remaining possibility, then, is that freedom of choice was given to the rational nature in order that it might preserve the rectitude of will it had received.

T: You have replied ably to the questions I asked. But we still need to investigate the purpose for which the rational nature ought to have preserved rectitude. Was it for the sake of rectitude itself, or for the sake of something else?

S: If freedom had not been given to that nature so that it might preserve rectitude of will for the sake of rectitude itself, freedom would not have been the capacity for justice, since it has been established[4] that justice is rectitude of will preserved for its own sake. But we believe that freedom of choice contributes to justice. Therefore, we must unhesitatingly assert that the rational nature received freedom for no other purpose than preserving rectitude of will for the sake of rectitude itself.

T: Therefore, since every freedom is a power, freedom of choice is the power to preserve rectitude of will for the sake of rectitude itself.

S: It can't be anything else.

T: So it is now clear that a free choice is nothing other than a choice that is able to preserve rectitude of will for the sake of rectitude itself.

S: It is indeed clear. Now as long as the rational nature had rectitude, it could preserve what it had. After it has abandoned rec-

3. In chapter 1.
4. In *DV* 12.

titude, however, how can it preserve what it does not have? Therefore, if there is no rectitude that can be preserved, there is no free
choice that can preserve it. For one cannot preserve what one does
not have.

T: Even if it lacks rectitude of will, the rational nature nonetheless has what is properly its own. For I believe we have no power
that by itself suffices for action. And yet even in the absence of
those things without which we can't exercise our powers at all,
we are nonetheless said to have those powers within ourselves.
In the same way, no instrument is sufficient by itself for any action or task;[5] and yet even in the absence of those things without
which we cannot make use of the instrument, we are nonetheless
correct to affirm that we have the instrument for some particular
action or task. And so that you can understand this in many cases,
I will show it to you in one: no one who has vision is said to be
entirely unable to see a mountain.

S: Someone who is unable to see a mountain certainly does not
have vision.

T: Then someone who has vision has the power and the instrument for seeing a mountain. And yet if there is no mountain there
and you say to him, "See the mountain," he will answer you, "I
can't, because there's no mountain there. If there were a mountain, I could see it." Similarly, if there were a mountain but no
light, and someone instructed him to look at the mountain, he
would reply that he couldn't, because there's no light; but if there
were light, then he could. Again, if both a mountain and light
were present to the person who has vision, but something were
interfering with his vision (say, if someone were keeping his eyes
shut), he would say that he could not see the mountain; but if
nothing were interfering with his vision, then undoubtedly he
would have the power to see the mountain.

S: Everyone knows all that.

---

5. "Action or task" renders a form of the Latin *operari* (and later, *opus*).
These are broad terms that can refer to everything from painting a pic-
ture to entertaining an idea. Basically, to exercise any power one has is
to *operari*; and the exercise of that power, or the product of that exercise
of power, is an *opus*. Anselm makes no clear distinction here between a
power and an instrument, and he will soon speak of the power of vision
as the "instrument or power for seeing." Elsewhere he speaks of the
power of will as the "instrument for willing": see chapter 7 and Appendix B.

T: So do you see that the power of seeing some body* is one power in the one who sees, another power in the object to be seen, and another in the medium (that is, neither in the one seeing nor in the thing to be seen); and in the medium there is one power in something that gives aid to vision and another in something that does not impede vision (that is, when nothing that could impede vision actually does so)?

S: I see it clearly.

T: There are, then, these four powers. If any one of them is lacking, the other three cannot accomplish anything, either individually or all together. And yet when the other three are missing, we do not deny that a person who has vision has vision, or the instrument or power for seeing, or that the visible thing can be seen, or that light can aid vision.

Chapter 4

In what way those who do not have rectitude have the power to preserve rectitude

The fourth of these, however, is improperly* called a power. For the only reason we say that something that typically impedes vision gives the power of seeing when it does not impede vision is that it does not take away vision. But the power to see light consists in only three things, since in that case what is seen and what aids vision are the same. Doesn't everyone know this?

S: Certainly.

T: So when there's nothing there for us to see, we're in total darkness, and our eyes are closed or blindfolded, we still have the power to see any visible thing—so far as it pertains to us. What, therefore, is to prevent us from having the power to preserve rectitude of will for the sake of rectitude itself, even in the absence of rectitude, as long as we have reason, by which we can know rectitude, and will, by which we can retain it? For freedom of choice consists of reason and will.

S: You have convinced me that this power of preserving rectitude of will is always present in rational nature, and that this power was free in the choice of the first human being and the angels, from whom rectitude of will could not be taken away against their will.

Chapter 5

That no temptation compels anyone to sin against his will

But how is the choice of the human will *now* free in virtue of this power, given that quite often a person whose will is right abandons that rectitude against his will because he is compelled by temptation?

T: No one abandons rectitude except by willing to do so. Therefore, if 'against one's will' means 'unwillingly',[6] no one abandons rectitude against his will. For someone can be tied up against his will, since he is unwilling to be tied up; he can be tortured against his will, since he is unwilling to be tortured; he can be killed against his will, since he is unwilling to be killed; but he cannot will against his will, since he cannot will if he is unwilling to will. For everyone who wills, wills his own willing.

S: Then how is it that someone is said to lie against his will when he lies in order to avoid being killed, since he does not lie without willing to lie? For just as it is against his will that he lies, so also it is against his will that he wills to lie. And if it is against his will that he wills to lie, he is unwilling to will to lie.

T: Perhaps he is said to lie against his will because, when he so wills the truth that he lies only for the sake of his life, he both wills the lie for the sake of his life and does *not* will the lie for its own sake, since he wills the truth. And so he lies both willingly and unwillingly. For a will by which we will a thing for its own sake, as when we will health for its own sake, is different from a will by which we will a thing for the sake of something else, as when we will to drink wormwood for the sake of health. Hence, on the basis of these two wills it could perhaps be said that his lying is both against his will and not against his will. So when he is said to lie against his will because insofar as he wills the truth he does not will to lie, this is not inconsistent with my saying that no one abandons rectitude of will against his will; for in lying, he wills to abandon rectitude of will for the sake of his life. And in virtue of that will he does not abandon rectitude against his will; rather, he abandons it willingly—and that is the will of which we are speaking now. We are, after all, speaking of the will by which

6. *Nolens*: The word most naturally describes someone who performs an action grudgingly or prefers to act otherwise, but Anselm takes it here in the more precise sense of 'not willing the action in question'.

he wills to lie for the sake of his life, not of that by which he does not will the lie for its own sake.

Or in any event, he certainly lies against his will because it is against his will that he must either lie or be killed—that is, it is against his will that he is in this difficulty, so that of necessity one of these two possibilities must come about. For although it is necessary that he either lie or be killed, it is not necessary that he be killed, since he can avoid being killed if he lies; and it is not necessary that he lie, since he can avoid lying if he is killed. Neither of these is determinately a matter of necessity, since both are in his power. And so although it is against his will that he must either lie or be killed, it does not follow either that he lies against his will or that he is killed against his will.

There is another argument as well that is often used to explain why someone is said to do against his will, unwillingly, and from necessity what he nonetheless does willingly. If it would be difficult to do something, and so we don't do it, we say that we can't do it, and that we abandon it from necessity or against our will. And if it would be difficult to refrain from doing something, and so we do it, we claim to do it against our will, unwillingly, and from necessity. So in this sense someone who lies to avoid death is said to lie against his will, unwillingly, and from necessity, since he cannot avoid the lie without risking death. Therefore, just as someone who lies for the sake of his life is improperly* said to lie against his will, since he is willing to lie, so also it is not properly said that his *willing* to lie is against his will, since he does not will to lie otherwise than willingly. For just as when he lies, he wills that lying, so also when he wills to lie, he wills that willing.

S: I can't deny what you're saying.

T: Then in what way is that will not free, given that no external power[7] can bring it into subjection without its consent?

S: Can't we, by a similar argument, say that the will of a horse is free, since it willingly serves the bodily appetite?

T: The two cases are not similar. In the horse, the will does not subject itself; instead, being subjected naturally,* it always of necessity* serves the bodily appetite. In a human being, by contrast, as long as the will itself is right, it does not serve what it ought not to serve, and is not subjected to what it ought not to be subjected to, and it is not turned aside from rectitude by any external

---

7. External power: *aliena potestas* (and later, *aliena vis*). Literally, 'power belonging to something else'.

power, unless it willingly consents to what it ought not. And it has this consent, as is clearly seen, not naturally or of necessity, like the horse, but through itself.

S: You have met my objection about the will of the horse. Go back to where we were.

T: Will you deny that something is free from another thing if it cannot be compelled or prevented by that other thing unless it is willing to be?

S: I don't see how I could deny it.

T: Then also explain in what way an upright will is victorious and in what way it is vanquished.

S: To persevere in willing rectitude itself is for it to overcome; to will what it ought not is for it to be overcome.

T: I believe that unless the will itself is willing, temptation cannot keep an upright will from rectitude or compel it to do what it ought not, so that it wills against rectitude and wills what it ought not.

S: Nor can I see any reason to think that's false.

T: Then who can say that a will is not free for preserving rectitude, and free from temptation and sin, if no temptation can turn it aside from rectitude to sin (that is, to willing what it ought not) unless it is willing? Therefore, when it is overcome, it is not overcome by something else's power, but by its own.

S: What has been said shows that.

T: Don't you see that it follows from this that no temptation can overcome an upright will? For if it can, it has a power of overcoming and overcomes by its own power. But that can't be, since the will is overcome solely by its own power. Therefore, temptation cannot in any way overcome an upright will; and when we say that temptation can do this, we are speaking improperly.* For this expression simply means that the will can submit itself to temptation—just as when we say that a weak man can be overcome by a strong man, we are not speaking of his own power but of someone else's, since this simply means that the strong man has the power to overcome the weak.

Chapter 6

In what way our will is powerful against temptations, even though it seems weak

S: Even though I cannot find anything wrong with the arguments by which you make every assault subject to our will and do not permit any temptation to master it, I cannot pretend that there is no weakness in the will, which almost all of us experience when we are overcome by the vehemence of temptation. So unless you show how the power for which you've argued is consistent with the weakness that we feel, my mind can't be at ease with this question.

T: This weakness in the will of which you speak: in what do you think it consists?

S: In the fact that one cannot persevere in clinging to rectitude.

T: If it is because of its weakness that the will does not cling to rectitude, it is turned away from rectitude by some external power.

S: I grant that.

T: And what power is that?

S: The power of temptation.

T: That power does not turn the will away from rectitude unless the will itself wills what temptation has suggested.

S: That's true. But that temptation itself by its power compels the will to will what it has suggested.

T: How does it compel the will to will: in such a way that the will could in fact not will, but only with great difficulty; or in such a way that it is completely unable not to will?

S: Although I must admit that we are sometimes so beleaguered by temptations that it would be difficult for us not to will what they suggest, I can't say that they ever overwhelm us to such an extent that we are completely unable not to will what they tell us to will.

T: I don't know how one could say that. For if a human being wills to lie in order to avoid death and preserve his life for a time, who will say that it is impossible for him to will not to lie in order to avoid eternal death and live forever? Hence, you should no longer doubt that this powerlessness[8] to preserve rectitude, which you say we experience in our wills when we consent to temptations, is not a matter of impossibility but of difficulty. For we commonly say that we can't do something, not because it is impossible for us to do it, but because we can do it only with difficulty. But this difficulty does not destroy the will's freedom; it can assail, but it cannot defeat, an unwilling will. In this way, then, I think you can see how the power of the will, which is vin-

---

8. Powerlessness: *impotentia*, the same word that is generally translated 'weakness' in this chapter.

dicated by truthful reasoning, is consistent with the weakness that our humanity experiences. For just as difficulty in no way destroys the will's freedom, so also that weakness—which we say is in the will precisely because it cannot retain its rectitude without difficulty—does not take away the will's power to persevere in rectitude.

Chapter 7

How the will is more powerful[9] than temptation,
even when it is overcome by temptation

S: I can't at all deny what you have proved, but I also can't by any means affirm that the will is more powerful than temptation when it is overcome by temptation. After all, if the will to preserve rectitude were more powerful than the onslaught of temptation, the will, in willing what it retains, would resist temptation more powerfully than temptation would assail the will. For the only way I know my will is more or less powerful is that I will more or less powerfully. So when I will what I ought less powerfully than temptation urges me to do what I ought not, I don't see how temptation is not more powerful than my will.

T: I see that you've been misled by an equivocation on the word 'will'.

S: I would like to understand that equivocation.

T: 'Will' is said equivocally in much the same way as 'sight'. We use the word 'sight' to refer to the instrument for seeing, that is, the ray proceeding through the eyes by which we see light and things that are in light; we also use it to refer to the activity[10] of that instrument when we make use of it, that is, vision. Similarly, we use the word 'will' to refer to the instrument for willing, which is in the soul, and which we direct to willing this or that, just as we direct sight to seeing various things; and we also use it to refer to the exercise of the will that is the instrument for will-

9. More powerful: *fortior*. Anselm relies heavily in this chapter on the adjective *fortis* (strong, powerful) and various cognates, and ideally an English translation would stick with one word and its cognates. Unfortunately, considerations of English idiom make this impossible. So the reader should bear in mind that *fortis* is translated variously as 'strong', 'powerful', and 'forceful'; *fortius* as 'more powerfully' and 'more forcefully'; and *fortitudo* as 'strength' and 'force'.

10. Activity: *opus*. See note 5.

ing, just as we use the word 'sight' to refer to the exercise of the sight that is the instrument for seeing.[11] Now we have the sight that is the instrument for seeing even when we are not seeing anything, whereas the sight that is its activity is in us only when we are seeing something. Similarly, the will that is the instrument for willing is always in the soul, even when it is not willing anything—for example, when one is asleep—but we have the will that I am calling the exercise or activity of that instrument only when we are willing something. So the will that I am calling the instrument for willing is always one and the same, no matter what we will; but the will that is its activity is as multifarious as the many objects and occasions of our willing—just as the sight that we have even in darkness or with our eyes closed is always the same, no matter what we see, whereas the sight that is its activity, which is also called vision, is as various as the varied objects and occasions of our seeing.

S: I clearly understand and admire this distinction between two senses of 'will', and I think I now realize the error I fell into because I didn't know it. Still, go on with what you've begun.

T: Then since you understand that there are two wills, the instrument for willing and its activity, in which of these two do you think the strength of willing resides?

S: In the will that is the instrument for willing.

T: Suppose you know a man who is so strong that if he restrains a wild bull, the bull can't move, and you see him restraining a ram in such a way that the ram breaks free from his grasp. Will you think that he is less strong in restraining the ram than in restraining the bull?

S: I will judge that he is equally strong in either action, but I will acknowledge that he is not using his strength equally, since he acts more forcefully on the bull than on the ram. The man is strong because he has strength, whereas his action is called strong because it is done forcefully.

T: In the same way you must understand that the will I am calling the instrument for willing has an inseparable strength, insuperable by any external power, which it sometimes uses more and sometimes less in willing. Hence, it by no means abandons what it wills more forcefully when it is offered what it wills less forcefully; and when it is offered what it wills more forcefully, it im-

---

11. See Appendix B for a passage from *De concordia* in which Anselm distinguishes more clearly between three different senses of 'will'.

mediately lets go of what it does not will with equal force. And then the will—which we can call the activity of this instrument, since it is actively at work when it wills something—this will as activity, I say, is called more or less strong as the action is done more or less forcefully.

S: I must admit that what you have explained is quite clear to me now.

T: Then you see that when a human being assailed by temptation abandons his rectitude of will, he is not torn away from rectitude by any external power; rather, his will turns itself to that which he wills more forcefully.

Chapter 8

That not even God can take away rectitude of will

S: Can God, at any rate, take away rectitude from the will?

T: You must understand in what sense he can't. He can indeed reduce to nothing the whole substance that he has made from nothing, but he cannot take away rectitude from a will that has it.

S: I am very eager for you to offer an argument for this claim of yours, which I have never heard before.

T: We are speaking of the rectitude of will in virtue of which a will is called just: that is, rectitude that is preserved for its own sake. Now no will is just unless it wills what God wills it to will.

S: One that does not will this is clearly unjust.

T: Then for any will that preserves rectitude, its preserving rectitude of will for the sake of rectitude itself is the same as its willing what God wills it to will.

S: So one must acknowledge.

T: If God takes away this rectitude from someone's will, he does so either willingly or unwillingly.

S: He cannot do so unwillingly.

T: So if he takes away rectitude from someone's will, he wills what he does.

S: Undoubtedly.

T: So if he takes away rectitude from someone's will, he does not will that that person should preserve rectitude of will for the sake of rectitude itself.

S: That follows.

T: But it has already been settled that for everyone who preserves rectitude, preserving rectitude of will in this way is the same as willing what God wills him to will.

S: Even if that hadn't been settled, it would still be true.

T: Therefore, if God takes this much-discussed rectitude away from someone, he does not will that person to will what he wills him to will.

S: Nothing could be more logical, but nothing could be more impossible.

T: Therefore, nothing is more impossible than for God to take away rectitude of will. Nonetheless, he is said to do this when he does not prevent someone from abandoning rectitude. Moreover, the devil or temptation is said to take away rectitude, or to overcome the will and tear it away from the rectitude it possesses, because unless he promised[12] something or threatened to take away something that the will wills more than rectitude, the will would by no means turn itself away from the rectitude that it does in fact will to some extent.

S: What you say appears so evident to me that I don't think anything could be said against it.

Chapter 9
That nothing is freer than an upright will

T: And so you see that nothing is freer than an upright will, since no external power can take away its rectitude. If, when it wills to lie in order not to lose life or well-being, we say that it is compelled by fear of death or torture to abandon the truth, that is certainly not true. For it is not compelled to will life more than truth; but since an external power prevents it from preserving both, it chooses what it wills more. And certainly the will does so spontaneously,* and not against its will, although its being in a position where it must abandon one or the other is not spontaneous, but against its will. For it has no less strength for willing truth than for willing well-being, but it wills well-being more forcefully. For if it saw right before its eyes the eternal glory that it would immediately attain if it preserved the truth, and the torments of hell to which it would be given over without delay if it lied, there's no question that it would quickly be found to have strength enough to preserve the truth.

S: That's clearly true, since it would show greater strength for willing eternal well-being for its own sake, and truth for the sake of the reward, than for preserving temporal well-being.

12. Reading *promitteret* for *permitteret*.

Chapter 10

*How someone who sins is a slave to sin; and that it is
a greater miracle when God restores rectitude to someone
who abandons it than when he restores life to a dead person*

T: So rational nature always has free choice, since it always has
the power to preserve rectitude of will for the sake of rectitude
itself, although sometimes with difficulty. But once a free will
abandons rectitude because of the difficulty of preserving it, the
will is thereafter a slave to sin because of the impossibility of recovering rectitude through its own power. Thus it becomes "a
spirit going on its way and not returning" [Psalm 78:39], since
"one who commits sin is a slave to sin" [John 8:34]. Indeed, just
as no will before it had rectitude could acquire it unless God gave
it, so also, once it has abandoned the rectitude it received, it cannot regain it unless God restores it. And I think it is a greater
miracle when God restores to a will the rectitude it has abandoned than when he restores to a dead man the life he has lost.
For a body, in dying out of necessity, does not sin so as never to
regain life; but a will, in abandoning rectitude through its own
power, deserves always to lack rectitude. And if someone spontaneously* inflicts death upon himself, he does not take away
from himself what he was never going to lose; but someone who
abandons rectitude of will throws away what he ought always to
have preserved.

S: I see that what you are saying about the slavery by which
"one who commits sin is a slave to sin" [John 8:34], and about the
impossibility of recovering rectitude once it is abandoned unless
it is restored by him who first gave it, is entirely true; and it
should be ceaselessly contemplated by all to whom rectitude is
given, in order that they might always retain it.

Chapter 11

That this slavery does not take away freedom of choice

But with this claim you have quite dampened my excitement,
since I was thinking it was already firmly established that human beings always have freedom of choice. So I insist that you
explain this slavery to me, lest it might perhaps seem incompatible with freedom. For both this freedom and this slavery are in
the will, and in virtue of them a human being is free or a slave.

So if he is a slave, how is he free? Or if he is free, how is he a slave?

T: If you distinguish carefully, he is, without any inconsistency, both free and a slave when he does not have rectitude. After all, it is *never* in his power to acquire rectitude when he doesn't have it; but it is always in his power to preserve it when he does have it. Because he cannot return to rectitude from sin, he is a slave; because he cannot be torn away from rectitude, he is free. But he can be turned back from sin, and from slavery to sin, only by someone else, whereas he can be turned away from rectitude only by himself; and he cannot be deprived of his freedom either by himself or by someone else. For he is always by nature free to preserve rectitude if he has it, even when he does not have the rectitude that he might preserve.

S: I am satisfied with the compatibility you have shown between freedom and slavery, so that they can both exist in the same person at the same time.

Chapter 12

Why, when a human being does not have rectitude, we say that he is free, since rectitude cannot be taken away from him when he has it, rather than saying that one who has rectitude is a slave, since he cannot recover it by his own power when he does not have it

But I very much want to know why, when someone does not have rectitude, we say that he is free, since no one else can take it from him when he has it, rather than saying that when he does have it, he is a slave, since he cannot recover rectitude by his own power when he does not have it. For because he cannot return from sin, he is a slave; because he cannot be torn away from rectitude, he is free; and just as he can never be torn away from it if he has it, so also he can never return to it if he does not have it. Hence, just as he is always free, so also, it seems, he is always a slave.

T: This slavery is nothing other than the inability not to sin. For whether we call it the inability to return to rectitude or the inability to recover rectitude or have it again, a human being is a slave to sin only because, since he cannot return to rectitude or recover it or have it again, he is unable not to sin. By contrast, when he has rectitude, he does not have the inability not to sin. Therefore, when he has rectitude, he is not a slave of sin. But he always has the power to preserve rectitude, both when he has rectitude and when he does not; and so he is always free.

As for your asking why, when someone does not have rectitude, we say that he is free, since no one else can take it from him when he has it, rather than saying that when he does have rectitude, he is a slave, since he cannot recover it by his own power when he does not have it: that's like asking why, when the sun is not present, we say that someone has the power to see it, since he can see it when it *is* present, rather than saying that when the sun is present, he is unable to see it, since when it is not present he cannot himself cause it to be present. For even when the sun is not present, we have within ourselves the power of vision by which we see it when it is present; and in the same way, when rectitude of will is lacking in us, we nonetheless have within ourselves the aptitude for understanding and willing by which we can preserve it for its own sake when we have it. And when we have everything we need in order to see the sun except its presence, the only power we lack is the one that its presence confers upon us; and in the same way, when we lack rectitude, the only inability we have is the one that its absence causes in us. Therefore, human beings always have freedom of choice, but they are not always slaves of sin. They are slaves of sin only when they do not have upright wills.

S: If I had reflected carefully on what you said earlier when you divided the power of seeing into four powers,[13] I would not have been uncertain about this; so I acknowledge that I'm to blame for my uncertainty.

T: I will forgive you now if from here on out you will keep what we say in the forefront of your mind as much as will be necessary, so that we won't have to repeat it.

S: I appreciate your kindness. But don't be surprised if just one hearing should not be enough to keep these things, which I have not been used to thinking about, always clearly before my mind's eye.

T: Tell me whether you are still in doubt about anything in the definition of freedom of choice that we have offered.

13. In chapter 3.

Chapter 13

That 'the power to preserve rectitude of will for the sake of
rectitude itself' is a perfect definition of freedom of choice

S: There is one thing that still worries me a bit about the definition. We often have a power to preserve something, but the power
is not free in such a way that it cannot be impeded by any external force. So when you say that freedom of choice is the power to
preserve rectitude of will for the sake of rectitude itself, consider
whether perhaps we ought to add something to indicate that this
power is so free that it cannot be overcome by any force.

T: If the power to preserve rectitude of will for the sake of rectitude itself could sometimes be found apart from the freedom
that we have come to understand, it would be a good idea to add
what you say. But since the stated definition is perfect in terms of
genus* and differences,* so that it includes neither more nor less
than the freedom we are investigating, it cannot be understood
to need any addition or deletion. For 'power' is the genus of freedom. By adding 'to preserve' we distinguish it from every power
that is not a power to preserve, for example, a power to laugh or
to walk. By adding 'rectitude' we distinguish it from the power
to preserve gold or whatever else is not rectitude. By adding 'of
will' we distinguish it from the power to preserve the rectitude
of other things, such as a stick or an opinion. By the phrase 'for
the sake of rectitude itself' we distinguish it from the power to
preserve rectitude of will for the sake of something else, as when
rectitude is preserved for the sake of money, or naturally.* For a
dog preserves rectitude of will naturally when it loves its pup-
pies or its kindly master.

Therefore, since there is nothing in this definition but what is
necessary to include the freedom of choice of a rational will and
to exclude everything else, and freedom is sufficiently included
and everything else sufficiently excluded, our definition is surely
neither overly broad nor overly narrow. Do you think so?

S: It certainly seems perfect to me.

T: Then tell me whether you have any further questions about
this freedom, on the basis of which an action, be it good or bad, is
imputed* to someone—for that is the only freedom we are discussing now.

Chapter 14
How this freedom is divided

S: You still need to set out how this freedom is divided. For although freedom as defined in this way is common to every rational nature, God's freedom is very different from that of rational creatures, and theirs in turn differs from one creature to another.

T: There is a freedom of choice that is from itself, neither made by nor received from anyone else; it belongs to God alone. There is another freedom of choice that is made by and received from God; it belongs to angels and human beings. The freedom that is made or received either has rectitude that it preserves, or lacks rectitude. That which has rectitude has it either separably or inseparably. That which has rectitude separably belonged to all the angels before the good were confirmed and the bad fell, and it belongs now to all human beings before death who have rectitude. That which has rectitude inseparably belongs to elect angels and human beings—but to angels after the fall of the reprobate and to human beings after their death. Now that which lacks rectitude lacks it either recoverably or irrecoverably. That which lacks it recoverably belongs only to human beings in this present life who lack it, although many do not recover it. That which lacks it irrecoverably belongs to reprobate angels and human beings—but to angels after their fall, to human beings after this life.

S: With God's assent you have so completely explained the definition and division of freedom that I can't find anything else I need to ask about them.

On the Fall of the Devil

Chapters

Chapter 1

That "What do you have that you did not receive?"
is said even to the angels; and that nothing is from
God but good and being; and that every good
has being and every being is good

STUDENT: When the Apostle[1] says "What do you have that you did
not receive?": is he saying this only to human beings, or to angels
as well?

TEACHER: No creature has anything from itself. For if a thing
does not have itself from itself, how can it have *anything* from
itself? In short, since there are only two sorts of things—the Creator and what he created—whatever being anything has must be
either God's own being or created being.[2]

S: That is indeed clear.

T: But neither the Creator nor what he created can have their
being from any source other than God himself.[3]

S: That is no less clear.

T: So he alone has from himself whatever he has, and all other
things have nothing but what they have from him. And just as
what they have from themselves is nothing, so also what they
have from him is something.

S: I don't think it's obviously true that what other things have
from God is something. After all, who else brings it about that
the many things we see passing from being to nonbeing are not
what they used to be, even if they do not pass completely into
nothingness? And who causes what-is-not not to be, unless it is
he who causes everything that is to be? Similarly, if something is
only because God makes it, it must be the case that what-is-not is

---

1. That is, the Apostle Paul, in 1 Corinthians 4:7.

2. More literally, "In short, since nothing exists but the one being who
created and the things created by that one being, it is clear that nothing
at all can be had but the one who created and what he created." It sounds
odd to say that God and his creation "can be had," but Anselm adopts
this formulation because the argument takes off from a question about
what creatures *have*. Since (as he will go on to argue) God has his own
being from himself, it is proper to say that God "is had" by himself; since
creatures have whatever they are from God, it is proper to say that what
God creates "is had" by creatures.

3. More literally, "But neither the Creator nor what is created can be had
except from the Creator."

not only because God doesn't make it. Therefore, just as those things that are have from him their being something, so also those that are not, or that pass from being to nonbeing, seem to have from him their being nothing.

T: It is not only someone who causes what-is-not to be, or causes what-is not to be, who is said to cause something to be or not to be. Rather, someone who can cause something not to be but refrains from doing so is also said to cause something to be; and someone who can cause something to be but refrains from doing so is also said to cause something not to be. For example, it is not only someone who robs another who is said to cause him to be naked or not to be clothed, but also someone who can prevent the robber but fails to do so. But this is said properly* of the former, whereas it is said improperly of the latter. For when it is said of the latter that he caused someone to be naked or not to be clothed, this simply means that although he could have caused the man to remain clothed or not to be naked, he didn't do so.

It is in this way that God is said to do many things that he does not do, as when he is said to lead us into temptation[4] because he does not spare us from temptation even though he could, or to cause what-is-not not to be, since he does not cause it to be even though he could. But if you would consider the things that are when they pass into nonbeing, it is not God who causes them not to be. After all, not only does no other essence* exist unless God makes it, but what God has made cannot persist even for a moment unless God preserves it; therefore, when he stops preserving what he made, that which used to be does not return to nonbeing because God causes it not to be, but because he stops causing it to be. For when God, as if in anger,[5] destroys something and thereby takes away its being, its nonbeing is not from God. Rather, when God takes away its being, like something of his own that he has lent—something he made and preserved in order that the thing might be—it returns to the nonbeing that it had from itself and not from God before it was made. After all, if you ask for your cloak back from someone to whom you willingly lent it temporarily when he was naked, he does not have his nakedness from you; instead, when you take

---

4. Cf. Matthew 6:13, Luke 11:4: "Lead us not into temptation."

5. "As if in anger," because Anselm denies that God actually has any emotions. See Appendix A (*Proslogion* 8).

away what was yours, he returns to what he was before you clothed him.

So surely, just as whatever is from the supreme Good is good, and every good is from the supreme Good, so also whatever is from the supreme Being has being, and every being is from the supreme Being.[6] Therefore, since the supreme Good is the supreme Being, it follows that everything good has being and every being is good. So since nothing and nonbeing do not have being, they are not good. And so nothing and nonbeing are not from him from whom only good and being come.

S: I now see clearly that just as good and being come only from God, so also whatever comes from God is good and has being.

T: Now when we read in the holy scriptures, or when we say in conformity with them, that God causes evil or causes something not to be,[7] you must not in the least suppose that I deny the point being made in those words or find fault with its being said in that way. But we should not so much cling to the improper words that conceal the truth as diligently seek the proper truth that lies hidden in many forms of expression.

S: That would go without saying for anyone who isn't either stupid or dishonest.

T: Go back to what you started with, and consider whether it can be said not only to human beings but also to angels that they have nothing they did not receive.

S: It's quite clear that this is true of angels no less than of human beings.

Chapter 2

Why it seems that the devil did not receive perseverance because God did not give it

So it is clear that the angel who remained steadfast in the truth persevered because he had perseverance, that he had perseverance because he received it, and that he received it because God gave it. It follows, then, that the one who "did not remain steadfast in the truth" [John 8:44] did not persevere because he did not have perseverance, that he did not have perseverance because he

6. The word translated 'being' in this paragraph is *essentia*. See the Glossary entry for **essence*** (4).

7. As we read in Isaiah 45:7, for example: "I form the light, and create darkness: I make peace, and create evil: I the Lord do all these things."

did not receive it, and that he did not receive it because God did not give it. So then I want you to explain to me, if you can, what the angel's fault was. After all, he did not persevere because God did not give him perseverance, and he could have nothing but what God gave him. For I am certain—even though I don't see how it could be true—that his damnation by the supremely Just was just, and he could not have been damned justly apart from some fault.

T: Why do you think it follows that if the good angel received perseverance because God gave it, then the evil angel did not receive it because God did not give it?

S: Because if its being given to the good angel was the cause of its being received, I think its not being given to the evil angel must have been the cause of its not being received. Now if we posit that it was not given, I see that this necessarily entails that it was not received; and we all know that when we don't receive something we want, it's not the case that it isn't given because we don't receive it, but rather we don't receive it because it isn't given. Finally, everyone I've heard or read asking this question always (as far as I can remember) brings it to a point with the following argument: if the good angel received perseverance because God gave it, the evil angel did not receive it because God did not give it. And I don't recall ever seeing a rejoinder to that reasoning.

Chapter 3

That God did not give perseverance because the evil angel did not receive it

T: That reasoning has no force at all, since it's possible for not-giving not to be the cause of not-receiving, even if giving were always the cause of receiving.

S: So if we posit the not-giving, the not-receiving doesn't necessarily follow. Therefore, there can be receiving even if there is no giving.

T: That's not so.

S: I'd like you to show me an example that illustrates what you're saying.

T: If I offer you something and you receive it, I do not give it because you receive it, but rather you receive it because I give it, and the giving is the cause of the receiving.

S: Right.

T: What if I offer that very same thing to someone else and he doesn't receive it?[8] Is it the case that he doesn't receive it because I don't give it?

S: No, it seems that you don't give it because he doesn't receive it.

T: So in this case, not-giving is not the cause of not-receiving; and yet if I posit that I didn't give it, that causes it to follow that he didn't receive it. You see, for one thing to cause another is not the same as for the *positing* of a thing to cause something else to follow. For example, burning is not the cause of fire, but fire is the cause of burning; and yet if we posit that there is burning, this always causes it to follow that there is fire. For if there is burning, there must be fire.

S: I have to admit you're right.

T: Then I think you understand that even though you received because I gave, it does not therefore follow that the one who did not receive did not receive because I didn't give; and yet it does follow that if I didn't give, he didn't receive.

S: I do understand, and I am pleased that I understand.

T: Do you still doubt that just as the reason the angel who remained steadfast received perseverance is that God gave it, so also the reason God did not give perseverance to the angel who did not remain steadfast is that the angel did not receive it?

S: You haven't shown me that yet. All you have succeeded in proving is that just because the reason the good angel received perseverance is that God gave it, it doesn't *follow* that the reason the bad angel didn't receive it is that God didn't give it. If you intend to claim that in fact the reason God didn't give it to the bad angel is that the angel didn't receive it, I want to know why he didn't receive it. It was either because he wasn't able to or because he didn't will to. Now if he lacked either the power or the will to receive it, God did not give them to him, since if God had given them, the angel certainly would have had them. Therefore, since he could not have either the power or the will to receive perseverance unless God gave them to him, in what way did he sin by not receiving what God gave him neither the power nor the will to receive?

T: God did give him the will and the power to receive perseverance.

8. I.e., does not accept it, refuses it.

S: Then he received what God gave, and he had what he received.

T: He did indeed receive it and have it.

S: Then he received and had perseverance.

T: He didn't receive it, and therefore he didn't have it.

S: Didn't you say that God gave him, and that he received, the will and the power to receive perseverance?

T: I did. But I didn't say that God gave him the receiving of perseverance, only that God gave him the will and the power to receive perseverance.

S: Then if he had the will and the power, he received perseverance.

T: That doesn't follow necessarily.

S: I don't see why not, unless you'll explain it to me.

T: Have you ever begun something with the will and the power to complete it, but then you failed to complete it because your will had changed before you finished?

S: Often.

T: Then you had the will and the power to persevere in something in which you did not in fact persevere.

S: I did indeed have the will, but I didn't persevere in that will, and therefore I didn't persevere in the action.

T: Why didn't you persevere in that will?

S: Because I didn't will to persevere.

T: As long as you willed to persevere in the action, didn't you will to persevere in that will itself?

S: I can't deny it.

T: Then why do you say you didn't will to persevere in it?

S: I would reply again that I willed to persevere but didn't persevere in that will, except that I see this would go on forever, with you always asking the same question and me always giving the same reply.

T: That's why you shouldn't say, "I didn't will to persevere in that will because I didn't will to persevere in willing that will." Instead, when asked why you did not persevere in that action in which you had the will and the power to persevere, you can reply that it was because you didn't persevere in that will. If you are then asked why you didn't persevere in that will, you should adduce a different cause, namely the reason why this deficiency in your will came about, rather than saying that it was because you didn't persevere in willing that will. For the latter reply merely restates the very thing that is being asked about, that is, the fact that you didn't persevere in the will to persevere in that action.

S: I realize that I didn't see what I should say.

T: So tell me in one word what it is to persevere in doing something as far as the thing requires.

S: To *finish* doing it. For when someone perseveres in writing, we say that he finishes writing; and when someone perseveres in leading, we say that he finishes leading.

T: Then let's likewise say, even though the expression is not in common use, that to persevere in willing is to finish willing.[9]

S: Very well.

T: So when you did not finish doing what you had the will and the power to finish, why didn't you finish doing it?

S: Because I didn't finish willing it.

T: Then in the same way you must say that the devil, who received the will and the power to receive perseverance and the will and power to persevere, did not receive perseverance and did not persevere because he did not finish willing.

S: But then again I want to know why he didn't finish willing. After all, when you say he did not finish willing what he willed, that just amounts to saying that he no longer willed what he had once willed. So when he no longer willed what he had once willed, why did he not will it, unless it was because he did not have the will? I don't mean the will he had had before, when he willed it, but the will he didn't have when he didn't will it. Why, then, did he not have this will, unless it was because he didn't receive it? And why didn't he receive it, unless it was because God didn't give it?

T: Again I say that it's not the case that he didn't receive it because God didn't give it; instead, God didn't give it because he didn't receive it.

S: Explain that.

---

9. Anselm's procedure is much clearer in the Latin. In the first three instances Anselm took the verb and added the prefix *per*. Thus *facere* (to do) became *perficere* (to bring to completion), *scribere* (to write) became *perscribere* (to write in full), and *ducere* (to lead) became *perducere* (to lead to the destination). Anselm now proposes to do the same with the word *velle* (to will), thereby coining a new word, *pervelle*, which will mean "to will to the end, to will with complete perseverance." In the translation I have represented *per* by the verb 'to finish': thus, *perficere* is "to finish doing," *pervelle* "to finish willing," and so on.

T: He spontaneously* forsook the will he had. Now as long as he possessed what he later abandoned, he received his possessing it; and in the same way he could have received his always retaining what he abandoned. But since he abandoned it, he did not receive his always retaining it. Therefore, it was because he abandoned it that he did not receive his retaining it—and it's not the case that he didn't receive it because God didn't give it, but instead God didn't give it because he didn't receive it.

S: Who would not understand that it's not because he abandoned it that he didn't will to retain it, but rather it's because he didn't will to retain it that he abandoned it? For not willing to retain something one has is always prior to willing to abandon it; after all, someone wills to abandon something he has because he does not will to retain it. So I am asking if there was a reason why he did not will to retain what he had, other than God's not giving him the will to retain it.

T: Not willing to retain something is not always prior to willing to abandon it.

S: Explain to me when it isn't.

T: When you do not will to retain a thing, but rather to abandon it, for its own sake: for example, if a live coal is placed in your bare hand. In such a case, perhaps, your not willing to retain the thing is prior to your willing to abandon it, and you will to abandon it because you do not will to retain it. After all, before you have it you do not will to retain it, and yet you cannot will to abandon it except when you have it.

By contrast, when you have something that you do not will to retain, but only for the sake of something else, and that you will to abandon only for the sake of something else, and you more strongly will something else that you cannot have unless you abandon what you have: in that case your willing to abandon something is prior to your not willing to retain it. For example, when a miser wills to retain a coin, but he more strongly wills bread, which he cannot have unless he spends his coin, his willing to spend—that is, to abandon—the coin is prior to his not willing to retain it. He does not, after all, will to spend the coin because he does not will to retain it; rather, he does not will to retain it because in order to have bread, he must spend it. Moreover, before he has it, he wills to have it and to retain it; and while he has it, he in no way lacks the will to retain it, so long as he need not abandon it.

S: That's true.

T: Therefore, not willing to retain something is not always prior to willing to abandon it; instead, willing to abandon something is sometimes prior.

S: I can't deny it.

T: I therefore say that it was not because his will was faulty—God having failed to give him the will—that he did not will what and when he ought to have willed; but instead, by willing what he ought not, he cast out his good will when an evil will came to exist within him. Hence, it is not the case that he did not have or receive a persevering good will because God did not give it to him; but rather, God did not give it to him because he deserted that will by willing what he ought not, and by deserting it did not retain it.

S: I understand what you're saying.

Chapter 4

In what way he sinned and willed to be like God

T: Do you still doubt that it was not because he did not will to retain what he had that the devil abandoned it, but rather it was because he willed to abandon it that he did not will to retain it?

S: I don't doubt that that *could* be true, but you haven't yet convinced me that it really *is* true. So show me first what he willed to have that he did not have, so that he willed to abandon what he did have, as you illustrated in the case of the miser. Then, if there's no possible objection, I will acknowledge that I don't doubt it really is true.

T: You don't doubt that he did in fact sin, since a just God could not condemn him unjustly; but you are asking in what way he sinned.

S: Exactly.

T: If he had persevered in preserving justice, he would never have sinned or been wretched.

S: That is what we believe.

T: And no one preserves justice except by willing what he ought or abandons justice except by willing what he ought not.

S: No one would doubt that.

T: So he abandoned justice, and thus sinned, by willing something that he ought not to have willed at that time.

S: That follows, but I'm asking what it was he willed.

T: Whatever he had, he ought to have willed.

S: Certainly he ought to have willed what he had received from God, and he did not sin by willing it.

T: Then he willed something that he did not have and that he ought not to have willed at that time, just as Eve willed to be "like the gods"[10] before God willed that.

S: I cannot deny that that follows too.

T: Now he could not will anything but justice or something advantageous. For happiness, which every rational nature wills, consists in advantageous things.

S: We can see this to be true in ourselves, since we will nothing but what we think is either just or advantageous.

T: But he could not sin by willing justice.

S: That's true.

T: Therefore, he sinned by willing something advantageous that he did not have and ought not to have willed at that time, but that could have served to increase his happiness.

S: Clearly that is the only way in which he could have sinned.

T: I believe you understand that by inordinately willing something in addition to what he had received, he stretched out his will beyond the bounds of justice.

S: I now see clearly that he sinned both by willing what he ought not and by not willing what he ought. It is also evident that it was not the case that he willed more than he ought because he did not will to retain justice. On the contrary, he did not retain justice because he willed something else; and by willing that, he abandoned justice—as you showed in the case of the miser, the coin, and the bread.

T: Now when he willed this thing that God did not want him to will, he willed inordinately to be like God.

S: If God must be thought of as so unique that nothing else like him can be thought,[11] how could the devil will what he could not think? After all, he was not so dense that he didn't know that nothing else can be thought to be like God.

T: Even if he didn't will to be completely equal to God, but instead willed something less than equality with God that was contrary to God's will: by that very fact he willed inordinately to be

10. Cf. Genesis 3:5, where the serpent tells Eve, "You will be like the gods, knowing good and evil."

11. This expression recalls Anselm's description of God as "that than which nothing greater can be thought" in the *Proslogion*, beginning with chapter 2.

like God, since he willed something by his own will, which was not subjected to anyone else. For it is the prerogative of God alone to will anything by his own will in such a way that he does not follow any higher will.

S: That's true.

T: Now he did not merely will to be equal to God by presuming to have a will of his own; he willed to be even *greater* than God, in that he placed his own will above God's will by willing what God didn't want him to will.

S: That's quite clear.

T: I believe it's obvious to you now from the arguments offered above that the devil spontaneously* stopped willing what he ought and justly lost what he had, since he spontaneously and unjustly willed what he didn't have and what he ought not to have willed.

S: I think nothing could be more obvious.

T: So although the good angel received perseverance because God gave it, it's not the case that the evil angel did not receive it because God didn't give it; rather, God didn't give it because he didn't receive it, and he didn't receive it because he didn't will to receive it.

S: You have given such satisfactory answers to my questions that both the truth of your premises and the validity of your arguments are firmly fixed in my understanding.

Chapter 5

That before the fall of the evil angels, the good angels were able to sin

T: Do you think the good angels were likewise able to sin before the evil angels fell?

S: I think so, but I would like to understand this through reason.

T: You know for certain that if they were not able to sin, they preserved justice out of necessity* and not in virtue of their power. Therefore, they did not merit grace from God for remaining steadfast when others fell any more than they did for preserving their rationality, which they could not lose. Nor, if you consider the matter rightly, could they properly be called just.

S: That's what reason shows.

T: So suppose that those who fell had not sinned, even though they were able to. They would have been greater than the angels who were not able to sin, insofar as they would have been genuinely just and would have merited grace from God. Hence, it follows either that elect human beings will turn out to be better and greater than the good angels, or that the reprobate angels will not be adequately replaced, since the human beings who are received in their place will not be such as they themselves were going to be.[12]

S: I think both these conclusions must be utterly rejected.

T: Therefore, the good angels were able to sin before the fall of the evil angels, just as has been shown in the case of those who fell.

S: I don't see how else things could be.

---

12. This cryptic argument depends in part on Anselm's views in *Cur Deus Homo* (*Why God Became Man*), Book One, chapters 16–18, where he argues that some human beings will fill up the places in heaven that should have been occupied by the angels who fell. If those views are borne in mind, Anselm's argument here can be understood in the following reformulation. The bad angels were (obviously) able to sin. But what about the good angels? Either they too were able to sin, or they weren't. Suppose they weren't. Then their actions were neither just nor meritorious. But in that case, saved human beings would actually be *better* than the good angels, since human beings are able to sin and therefore can act justly and meritoriously. And we can't say that human beings are better than angels. So suppose instead we cling to the view that saved human beings are *not* better than the good angels. It would follow that human beings, like the good angels, act neither justly nor meritoriously. But that can't be true either, since saved human beings are supposed to fill up the gap left by the desertion of the evil angels. Now those evil angels were able to sin, which means that if they *hadn't* sinned, they would have acted justly and meritoriously. If saved human beings do not act justly and meritoriously, they are not fitting replacements for the rebel angels ("they will not be such as [the reprobate angels] were going to be"). Therefore, since the assumption that the good angels were unable to sin leads to all sorts of dead ends and absurdities, we must conclude that they were able to sin.

Chapter 6

How the good angels have been confirmed in their
steadfastness and the evil angels in their fall

T: And so the good angels willed the justice that they had rather
than that additional something which they didn't have. As far as
their own will was concerned, they lost that good (as it were) for
the sake of justice; but they received it as a reward for justice, and
they remained forever in secure possession of what they had.
Hence, they have progressed so far that they have attained everything they could will, and they no longer see what more they
could will; and because of this they are unable to sin. By contrast,
the evil angels willed that additional something which God did
not yet will to give them, rather than willing to remain steadfast
in the justice in which they were created. By the judgment of that
very justice, they not only failed utterly to obtain that on account
of which they scorned justice but also lost the good they had.
Therefore, the angels are distinguished in the following way:
those who cleave to justice can will no good that they do not enjoy, and those who abandon justice can will no good that they do
not lack.

S: Nothing could be more just or more beautiful than this distinction. But if you can tell me, I would like to hear what sort of
advantageous thing this was that the good angels justly spurned
and thereby advanced, and the evil angels unjustly desired and
thereby fell away.

T: I don't know what it was. But whatever it might have been,
all we need to know is that it was something they were able to
attain, which they did not receive when they were created, in order that they might advance to it by their own merit.

S: And let this be enough for our discussion of this point.

Chapter 7

Questions: Is the will, and its turning to what it ought
not, the very evil that makes them evil? And why can't
the rational creature turn from evil to good on its own,
as it can turn from good to evil on its own?

But I don't know what it is—as soon as I hope I've finally answered one question, I see more questions sprouting up from the

roots of those I've already mowed down. Now that I quite clearly see that unrestrained concupiscence was the only reason the rebel angel could have fallen into this extreme lack of anything good, I am very troubled about the source of this inordinate will. For if that will was good, then it was on account of a good will that he fell from such great good into such great evil. Moreover, if it was good, then God gave it to him, since he had nothing from himself. So if he willed what God gave him to will, what was his sin? On the other hand, if he had this will from himself, he had something good that he did not receive.

Now if that will is evil and is also something, the problem arises again: his evil will must have been from God, who is the source of whatever is something. And once again one can ask what his sin was in having the will God gave him, or how God could give an evil will. If, however, this evil will was from the devil himself and is also something, then the devil had something from himself, and not every essence* is good; nor will evil be nothing, as we are accustomed to say, since an evil will is an essence. On the other hand, if an evil will is nothing, it was on account of nothing, and therefore without cause, that he was so harshly condemned. And what I'm saying about will can equally well be said about concupiscence or desire, since both concupiscence and desire are will; and just as there is good and evil will, so also there is good and evil concupiscence and good and evil desire.

Now suppose someone said that a will is an essence* and is therefore something good, but that it becomes a good will by turning to what it ought but is called a bad will when it turns to what it ought not. Then I notice that whatever I said about the will can be said about this turning of the will. For I am very troubled about the source of the perverse turning of the devil's will, and about the other things I said just now about the will. And there is still something else that bewilders me whenever I think about this turning of the will, namely, why God made that excellent and sublime nature such that it could turn its will from what it ought to will to what it ought not to will but could not turn from what it ought not to will to what it ought. For it seems that such a creature ought to have received from such a Creator the power to do the good for which it was created, rather than the evil it was created to avoid. The same question can be asked about our own nature, since we believe that no human being can have a good will unless God gives it, whereas we can have an evil will at any time if God merely permits it.

Chapter 8

*That neither the will nor its turning is the very evil
that makes them evil*

T: I don't think we can deny that both the will and its turning are
something. For even if they are not substances,* it still cannot be
proved that they are not essences,* since there are many essences
besides those that are properly* called substances. Moreover, a
good will is no more a something than is a bad will, nor is a bad
will more an evil than a good will is a good. For a merciful, generous will is no more a something than a merciless, rapacious
will; nor is the latter more an evil than the former is a good.
Therefore, if an evil will is the very evil because of which someone is called evil, it would follow that a good will is the very good
by which someone is made good. But then it would turn out that
an evil will is nothing at all, if it is that very evil that we believe
to be nothing; and then a good will would also be nothing, since
it is no more a something than an evil will is. So we would be
forced to hold that the very good that makes beings good is nothing, since it is the good will, which would be nothing. But no one
for a moment supposes that a good will, or good itself, is nothing. Therefore, an evil will is not the very evil that makes beings
evil, just as a good will is not the very good that makes them
good.

Now what I said about the will can also be applied to the will's
turning: the turning by which a will turns from stealing to be-
stowing is no more a something than that by which the very same
will turns from generosity to greed. And so on, for all the things I
said about the will a moment ago.

S: What you say seems right to me too.

T: Therefore, neither the evil will nor the wicked turning of the
will is the very evil that makes an angel or a human being evil—
i.e., the very evil that we claim is nothing—nor is the good will
or the good turning of the will the good that makes them good.

Chapter 9

That injustice is that very evil and is nothing

S: Then what are we to say is the very evil that makes them evil,
and what is the very good that makes them good?

T: We ought to believe that justice is the very good in virtue of which both angels and human beings are good, that is, just, and in virtue of which the will itself is said to be good or just; whereas injustice is the very evil that we claim is nothing other than a privation of good, which makes them and their will evil. And consequently, we hold that injustice is nothing other than the privation of justice. For when a will was initially given to the rational nature, it was, simultaneously with that giving, turned by the Giver himself to what it ought to will—or rather, it was not turned but *created* upright. Now as long as that will remained steadfast in the rectitude in which it was created, which we call truth or justice, it was just. But when it turned itself away from what it ought to will and towards what it ought not, it did not remain steadfast in the original rectitude (if I may so call it) in which it was created. When it abandoned that rectitude, it lost something great and received in its place nothing but its privation, which has no essence,* and which we call 'injustice'.

Chapter 10
How evil seems to be something

S: I grant what you say about evil's being a privation of good, but I equally see that good is a privation of evil. And just as I perceive that in the privation of evil something else comes about that we call 'good', so also I notice that in the privation of good something else comes about that we call 'evil'. Now there are certain arguments proving that evil is nothing. For example, it has been argued that evil is nothing but a flaw or corruption, which exists only in some essence,* and the more flaws and corruptions there are in an essence, the more they reduce it to nothingness; and if that essence falls completely into nothingness, the flaws and corruptions will also be found to be nothing. But even if this or some other argument is offered to show that evil is nothing, my mind cannot endorse that view, except by faith alone, unless someone refutes my contrary argument proving that evil is something. For when we hear the name[13] 'evil', there would be no rea-

---

13. *Nomen*: I have chosen to translate *nomen* consistently as 'name', since that makes the best sense of Anselm's arguments on the whole; but readers should bear in mind that *nomen* can also have the more general meaning 'word' and the narrower meaning 'noun'.

son for our hearts to fear what they understand to be signified by that name if in fact it signified nothing. Moreover, if the word 'evil' is a name, it surely has a signification; and if it has a signification, it signifies. But then it signifies *something*. How, then, is evil nothing, if what the name 'evil' signifies is something? Finally, consider what peace there is, what rest, while justice endures: so that in many cases it seems that justice, like chastity and forebearance, is nothing but restraint from evil. But when justice is gone, what varied, troublesome, and multifarious feelings take possession of the soul; like a cruel master they force their wretched slave to be anxious about so many depraved and wearisome deeds and to labor so painfully in doing them. It would be astonishing if you could show that *nothing* accomplishes all this.

Chapter 11

That one cannot prove on the basis of the names
that evil and nothing are something, but rather
that they are quasi-something

T: I imagine you're not crazy enough to say that *nothing* is something, even though you cannot deny that 'nothing' is a name. So, if you cannot prove that nothing is something based on the name 'nothing', how do you think you're going to prove that evil is something based on the name 'evil'?

S: An example that resolves one controversial issue by bringing in another is useless. For I don't know what nothing is, either. So, since the question at hand concerns the evil that you say is nothing, if you want to teach me what I should understand evil to be, first teach me what I should understand nothing to be; and then you will respond to the other considerations, besides the name 'evil', that I said induced me to think evil is something.

T: Now given that there is no difference at all between being nothing and not being something, how can one say what that which is not something *is*?

S: If there isn't something that is signified by the name 'nothing', then that name doesn't signify anything; and if it doesn't signify anything, it's not a name. But surely it *is* a name. Therefore, although no one would say that nothing is something, but instead we must always say that nothing is nothing, still, no one can deny that the name 'nothing' has a signification. But if this name does not signify nothing, but instead signifies something, then it seems that what it signifies cannot be nothing but instead is something. Therefore, if what it signifies is not nothing but instead is something, how will it be true that this word signifies that which is nothing? After all, if 'nothing' is said truly, then what is signified by the name is truly nothing, and therefore it isn't something. Hence, if what is signified by this name is not nothing but instead is something—as the argument seems to show—then it is falsely and inappropriately called by that name. But on the other hand, if (as everyone agrees) that which is named 'nothing' truly is nothing and in no way is something, could anything at all follow more logically than this: that this word signifies nothing, that is, doesn't signify anything? And so why is it that the name 'nothing' does not signify nothing but instead something, and also does not signify something but instead nothing?

T: Perhaps signifying nothing is not inconsistent with signifying something.

S: Suppose they're not inconsistent. Then either this word signifies nothing when taken in one way and something when taken in another way, or else we will have to find a thing that is both something and nothing.

T: What if both turn out to be true? That is, what if we can find two ways of understanding this name and also find one and the same thing to be both something and nothing?

S: I would like to know both.

T: It is agreed that as far as its signification goes, the word 'nothing' is in no way different from 'not-something'. And nothing is more obvious than this: 'not-something' by its signification requires that every thing whatsoever, and anything that is something, is to be excluded from the understanding, and that no thing at all or what is in any way something is to be included in the understanding. But since there is no way to signify the exclusion of something except by signifying the very thing whose exclusion is signified—for no one understands what 'not-human' signifies except by understanding what a human is—the expression 'not-something' must signify something precisely by eliminating that which is something. On the other hand, by excluding everything that is something, it signifies no essence* that it requires to be included in the hearer's understanding. Therefore, the expression 'not-something' does not signify any thing or that which is something.

Therefore, the expression 'not-something' under different aspects both in some way signifies a thing and something, and in no way signifies a thing or something. For it signifies by excluding; it does not signify by including. The same argument applies to the name 'nothing', which excludes everything that is something: by what it eliminates, it signifies something rather than nothing, and by what it includes, it signifies nothing rather than something. Therefore, it is not necessary that nothing be something just because its name signifies something in a certain way; but rather, it is necessary that nothing be nothing, because its name signifies something in that particular way. And so in this way it is not inconsistent for evil to be nothing and yet for the name 'evil' to have a signification, given that it signifies something by excluding it and does not include any thing.

S: I can't deny that the name 'nothing' in some way signifies something, as you've just argued; but it is quite well-known that the something that is signified in that way by this name is not named 'nothing'. Nor when we hear this name do we take it as standing for the thing that it signifies in that way. So I am asking about the item[14] that we use this name to stand for and that we understand when we hear this name—I mean, I'm asking what that item is. After all, it is what this name properly* signifies; this name is a name because it signifies that item, not because it signifies something by denying, in the way you explained earlier. That name is reckoned among names precisely because it signifies that item, and that item is called 'nothing'. I am asking how that item is something if it is properly called 'nothing', or how it is nothing if the name that signifies it signifies something, or how one and the same item is both something and nothing. I ask the same questions about the name 'evil', both about what it signifies and about what is named 'evil'.

T: You are right to ask these questions, since even though the argument given above shows that 'evil' and 'nothing' signify something, what they signify is not evil or nothing. But there is another argument showing that they signify something and that

14. There is no word in the Latin corresponding to 'item'. I use it to avoid a confusing string of neuter pronouns with different referents in the sentences that follow. 'Thing' would not work, because the student is not committed to the notion that whatever is referred to by 'nothing' qualifies as a thing; indeed, he is committed to just the opposite, which is why he avoids words like 'something' and 'thing' and formulates his question using only neuter demonstrative pronouns.

what they signify is something—yet not really something, but quasi-something.

You see, the form of an expression often doesn't match the way things are in reality.[15] For example, 'to fear' is active according to the form of the word even though fearing is passive in reality. And in the same way, 'blindness' is something according to the form of the expression, even though it is not something in reality. For we say that someone has blindness and that there is blindness in him in just the same way that we say someone has vision and that there is vision in him, even though blindness is not something, but instead not-something, and to have blindness is not to have something but rather to lack that which is something. After all, blindness is nothing other than non-vision or the absence of vision where there ought to be vision; and non-vision or the absence of vision is not something in cases where there ought to be vision any more than it is in cases where there ought not to be vision. Therefore, blindness is not something in the eye, just because there ought to be vision in the eye, any more than non-vision or the absence of vision is something in a stone, where there ought not to be vision. And there are many other similar cases in which things that are not something are called something according to the form of the expression, in that we speak of them as we speak of things that really exist.

It is in this way, then, that 'evil' and 'nothing' signify something; and what they signify is something, not in reality, but according to the form of the expression. For 'nothing' does not signify anything other than not-something, or the absence of those items that are something. And evil is not anything other than not-good, or the absence of good where it is required or fitting that good should be. Now that which is not anything other than the absence of what is something is certainly not itself something. Therefore, evil is truly nothing, and nothing is not something; and yet in a certain way evil and nothing *are* something, because we speak of them as if[16] they were something when we say, "He did nothing" or "He did evil," or "What he did is nothing" or "What he did is evil," in the same way in which we say "He did something" or "He did what is good," or "What he did is something" or "What he did is good." That's why, when we utterly deny that

---

15. Literally, "many things are said according to form that are not so in reality."

16. "As if": Latin, *quasi*; hence the expression "quasi-something" above.

what someone says is something, we say "That which you say is nothing." For 'that' and 'which' are properly said only of that which is something; and when they are used in the expression I just mentioned, they are not said of that which is something, but of that which is spoken of as if it were something.

S: You have succeeded in meeting the argument based on the name 'evil' by which I thought I could prove that evil is something.

Chapter 12

That the angel could not have his first will from himself; and that 'can' is applied to many things because of something else's power and 'cannot' because of something else's lack of power

You still need to show me how I can reply to the other considerations that strive to persuade me that evil is something.[17]

T: In order for us to be able to elucidate the truth of the matter, we will have to begin a little further back. But it's important for you not to be content merely to understand each of the things I say individually, but to gather them all up in your memory at the same time and see them in one glance, as it were.

S: I will be as attentive as I can. But if I prove to be somewhat slower than you might wish, don't become annoyed at having to wait for me as you see that my slowness requires it.

T: Well, let's suppose that right now God is making an angel that he wills to make happy, and he's not making the angel all at once, but rather part by part. Up to this point the angel has been made apt to have a will, but he does not yet will anything.

S: Suppose whatever you like, and explain what I am asking about.

T: Do you think this angel can will anything on his own?

---

17. "The other considerations" are those raised in the last three sentences of chapter 10. They are finally answered in chapter 26. As the teacher indicates in his next speech, chapters 12 through 25 set up the philosophical account needed to make the claims of chapter 26 compelling, and those chapters should be read with the considerations of chapter 10 in mind. This is not to say, of course, that chapters 12 through 25 are interesting *only* for the light they shed on the problem raised in chapter 10; on the contrary, they are arguably the philosophical centerpiece of *DCD*.

S: I don't really understand what you mean by 'on his own'. For as you said earlier,[18] no creature has anything that it did not receive, and no creature can do anything on its own.

T: By 'on his own' I mean in virtue of what he already has. For example, someone who has feet and whatever else suffices for the ability to walk can walk on his own, whereas someone whose feet are injured cannot walk on his own. This is the sense in which I am asking whether the angel who is already apt to will but does not yet will anything can will something on his own.

S: I think he can, if at some point he wills.

T: You're not answering my question.

S: How so?

T: My question is about someone who is willing nothing, and about the possibility[19] that precedes the fact; but your answer is about someone who wills, and about the possibility that comes about with the fact. For whatever is, by the very fact that it is, can be. But not everything that is could be before it was. So when I ask whether this angel who wills nothing can will, I am asking about the possibility before he wills, by which he can move himself to will; but when you reply that if he wills, he can will, you are talking about the possibility that comes about with that will itself. For necessarily, if he wills, he can will.

S: I know that there are two possibilities, one that is not yet realized in fact, and one that is already realized in fact. But I also can't help but know this: if anything can be in the sense that it now actually exists, then if at any time it did not exist, it previously could exist. After all, if it could not have existed, it would never have existed. So I think my reply was perfectly adequate: since, given that he wills, he can will, it must be the case that before he willed, he could will.

T: Do you think that what is nothing has nothing at all and therefore has no power,[20] and that without power there is absolutely nothing it can do or be?

---

18. In chapter 1.

19. Possibility: *potestas*, the abstract noun corresponding to the verb *posse*, which I have been translating 'can'.

20. Power: again, *potestas*. Part of Anselm's point in this chapter is to distinguish two senses of *potestas*: to say that *x* has the *potestas* to be *y* might just mean that it is possible for *x* to be *y*, but it might mean something more, namely, that *x* can bring it about that *x* is *y*. (Consider two examples: a banana has the *potestas* to be digested in the first sense but

S: I can't deny that.

T: I believe that before the world was made, it was nothing.

S: You're right.

T: Therefore, before it existed, there was nothing it could do or be.

S: That follows.

T: Therefore, before it existed, it could not exist.

S: And I say that if it could not exist, it was impossible for it ever to exist.

T: That was both possible and impossible before it existed. It was impossible for the world, since the world did not have the power to exist; but it was possible for God, who had the power to make the world. Therefore, the world exists because before it was made, God could make it, not because before it existed the world itself could exist.

S: I can't rebut your argument, but our normal way of speaking is against you.

T: That's not surprising. Many things are said improperly* in ordinary speech; but when it is incumbent upon us to search out the heart of the truth, we must remove the misleading impropriety to the greatest extent possible and as much as the subject matter demands. Because of such impropriety in speaking we quite often apply the word 'can' to a thing, not because it can do anything, but because something else can; and we apply the word 'cannot' to a thing that can do something, simply because some other thing cannot. For example, if I say "a book can be written by me," the book certainly can't do anything, but I can write the book. And when we say "This man cannot be defeated by that man," we understand this to mean simply, "That man cannot de-

---

not in the second, since it cannot throw itself into your intestines and bombard itself with digestive enzymes and so forth. By contrast, I have the *potestas* to be in Chicago in both senses: it is possible for me to be in Chicago, and I myself have the power to bring it about that I am in Chicago.) The problem is that in English we have a ready-made distinction between these two senses. For the first we use 'possibility', and for the second we use 'power'. Anselm must therefore labor to make clear a distinction we already have firmly entrenched in ordinary language. The analogue in English would be to distinguish between two uses of 'can': when I say that the banana can be digested, I am using a sense of 'can' that implies mere possibility; but when I say that I can be in Chicago, I am using a sense of 'can' that implies a power.

feat this man."[21] This is why we say that God cannot undergo anything harmful to himself or do anything wicked, since he is so powerful in his blessedness and justice—or rather, since in him blessedness and justice are not distinct things but a single good, he is so all-powerful in his unitary good—that no thing can do what would harm the supreme Good. Hence, he can neither be corrupted nor lie.[22]

Therefore, whatever does not exist cannot, before it exists, exist through its own power; but if some other thing can cause it to exist, then it can exist through something else's power. Now although there are many ways to draw distinctions involving power or lack of power, let this be enough for now: 'can' is applied to many things not because of their own power, but because of something else's power; and 'cannot' is applied to many things not because of their own lack of power, but because of something else's lack of power. So I am speaking of his own power when I ask about the newly created angel whom we are imagining, who up to this point has been made apt to have a will but does not yet will anything. Can he will anything on his own? Answer in terms of his own power.

S: If he is already apt to will and lacks nothing but the willing itself, I don't see why he can't will on his own. After all, someone who is apt to see, but doesn't see anything, who is placed in the light but with his eyes closed, can see on his own. Why, then, couldn't someone who is not willing will on his own in the same way that someone who is not seeing can see on his own?

T: Because the one who is not seeing has vision and a will by which he can move vision. We, however, are speaking of an angel who has no will. So answer this question: if a thing moves itself from not willing to willing, does it will to move itself?

S: If I say that it is moved without willing, what will follow is that it is moved by something else rather than by itself—except perhaps if someone suddenly closes his eyes in anticipation of a blow or is compelled by something disadvantageous to will what he did not will before. For in those cases I'm not sure whether he first moves himself to this will.

T: No one is compelled by fear or the expectation of something disadvantageous, or incited by love of something advantageous, to will something, unless he first has a natural* will to avoid what

21. Cf. *DV* 8.
22. Cf. Appendix C (*Proslogion* 7).

is disadvantageous or have what is advantageous. By that will he moves himself to other wills.

S: I can't deny that.

T: You must acknowledge, therefore, that whatever moves itself to will, first wills to move itself.

S: Yes.

T: Therefore, that which wills nothing can in no way move itself to will.

S: I can't object.

T: So it must be the case that the angel who has already been made apt to have a will but nonetheless does not will anything cannot have his first will from himself.

S: I have to grant you that, since that which wills nothing can will nothing on its own.

T: Now he cannot be happy unless he wills happiness. By 'happiness' I don't mean happiness in accordance with justice, but the happiness that everyone wills, even the unjust. After all, everyone wills his own well-being. For leaving aside the fact that every nature* is said to be good, we commonly speak of two goods, and of two evils that are contrary to them. One good is that which is called "justice," whose contrary evil is injustice. The other good is what I think can be called "the advantageous"; its opposite evil is the disadvantageous. Now not everyone wills justice, and not everyone avoids injustice, whereas not merely every rational nature, but indeed everything that can be aware of it wills the advantageous and avoids the disadvantageous. For no one wills anything unless he thinks it is in some way advantageous for himself. So in this way everyone wills his own well-being and wills against his own unhappiness. It is of happiness in this sense that I said just now that no one can be happy unless he wills happiness. For no one can be happy either in having what he does not will or in not having what he does will.

S: There's no denying that.

T: And someone who does not will justice *ought* not to be happy.

S: That's equally true.

Chapter 13

That, having received only the will for happiness, he would
not be able to will anything else
or to refrain from willing happiness; and that no matter
what he might will,
his will would be neither just nor unjust

T: Then let's say that God first gives him only the will for happiness and see whether, in virtue of having received a will, he is now able to move himself to will something other than happiness.[23]

S: Continue what you have begun. I'm ready to understand.

T: It is agreed that he does not yet will anything besides happiness, since he has not received the will for anything else.

S: That's true.

T: So I'm asking you whether he can move himself to will something else.

S: I can't see how someone who wills nothing besides happiness would move himself to will anything other than happiness. After all, if he wills to move himself to will something else, he wills something else.

T: Therefore, just as he could not will anything at all on his own when no will had yet been given him, so also he cannot have any other will from himself if he has received only the will for happiness.

S: Yes.

T: What if he thought something would contribute to his attaining happiness? Couldn't he move himself to will that?

S: I'm not sure how to reply. If he can't, I don't see how he's willing happiness, since he can't will that through which he thinks he can attain happiness. On the other hand, if he can, I don't understand in what sense he can't will anything other than happiness.

T: If someone wills something, not for the sake of the thing he appears to will, but for the sake of something else, which should one properly* judge him to be willing: that which he is said to will, or that for the sake of which he wills?

S: Surely that for the sake of which he seems to will.

23. "Other than happiness": literally, "other than what he received to will."

T: So someone who wills something for the sake of happiness is not willing anything other than happiness. Therefore, it can be true both that he wills what he thinks will contribute to his happiness and that he wills only happiness.

S: That's quite clear.

T: I still want to know whether, having received only this will, he can refrain from willing happiness.

S: He cannot simultaneously both will it and refrain from willing it.

T: That's true, but it's not what I'm asking. I'm asking whether he can abandon that will and move himself from willing happiness to refraining from willing it.

S: If he does that unwillingly, it is not he who is doing it. On the other hand, if he does it willingly, he is willing something other than happiness. But he *doesn't* will anything other than happiness. So I think it's obvious that there's no way he can, on his own, will anything other than the one thing he received the power to will.[24]

T: You have understood this well. But now tell me whether someone who wills nothing other than happiness, and who cannot refrain from willing happiness, can keep from willing happiness more and more, the greater he understands it to be.

S: If he didn't will happiness more and more, the greater and better he understood it to be, then either he wouldn't be willing happiness at all, or else he would will something else on account of which he would not will the better thing.[25] But we are supposing that he wills happiness and nothing else.

T: Then the higher he realizes happiness can be, the more he wills to be happy.

S: Undoubtedly he does.

T: Therefore, he wills to be like God.

S: Nothing could be more obvious.

T: What do you think: would his will be unjust if he willed in this way to be like God?

S: I don't want to call him just, since he would be willing what is not fitting; nor do I want to call him unjust, since he would be willing out of necessity.

T: Now we said that someone who wills only happiness wills only advantageous things.

24. "Received the power to will": literally, "received to will."
25. I.e., happiness.

S: Yes.

T: Then suppose someone who willed nothing but advantageous things could not have those that are greater and truer. Would he will lesser things—whichever ones he could make use of?

S: Indeed, he could not refrain from willing any of the very lowest, if he couldn't have greater ones.

T: Since he would will the lowest advantageous things, the impure things in which irrational animals take pleasure, wouldn't his will be unjust and blameworthy?

S: How would his will be unjust or deserve reproach, given that it would be willing what it did not receive the power not to will?

T: And yet it is well-established that his will, whether it wills the highest advantageous things or the lowest, is the work and gift of God, just as his life and his power of sensation are, and that there is neither justice nor injustice in it.

S: Undoubtedly.

T: Therefore, insofar as it is an essence,* it is something good; but as far as justice and injustice are concerned, it is neither good nor bad.

S: Nothing could be clearer.

T: But he ought not to be happy if he does not have a just will. Indeed, someone who wills what neither can nor ought to be the case cannot be either completely or commendably happy.

S: That is quite evident.

Chapter 14

That the case would be similar if he had received only the will for rectitude, and that he received both wills simultaneously in order that he might be both just and happy

T: Then let's consider the will for justice. If this same angel were given only the will for what it is fitting that he will, could he will anything else? And could he refrain on his own from willing justice?[26]

S: What we found regarding the will for happiness must also turn out to be completely true of this will too.

---

26. "Willing justice": literally, "willing what he had received to will."

T: Therefore, he would not have either a just or an unjust will. For just as, if he were given only the will for happiness, his will would not be unjust even if he willed unfitting things, since he would not be able to refrain from willing them, so also if he were given only the will for justice, his will would not be just simply because he willed what is fitting, since he would have received that willing in such a way that he would not be able to will otherwise.

S: That's right.

T: Therefore, since he cannot be called just or unjust for willing only happiness or for willing only what is fitting when he wills in that way out of necessity, and since he neither can nor ought to be happy unless he wills to be happy and wills it justly, God must create both wills in him in such a way that he both wills to be happy and wills it justly. This added justice governs his will for happiness so as to curtail its excess without eliminating its power to exceed. Thus, since he does will to be happy, he can exceed the limits of justice, but since he wills it justly, he does not will to exceed them. And thus, having a just will for happiness, he both can and ought to be happy. By refraining from willing what he ought not to will, even though he could will it, he deserves to be unable ever to will what he ought not; and by always retaining justice through a disciplined will, he deserves not to lack happiness in any way. On the other hand, if he abandons justice through an undisciplined will, he deserves to be deprived of happiness altogether.

S: I cannot imagine anything more fitting.

T: Remember that earlier, when we were examining the will for happiness by itself, without the restraint we added so that it might subject itself to God, we said there would be no justice or injustice in it no matter what it willed.

S: I remember that well.

Chapter 15

That justice is something

T: Now do you think that this item which, when added to the will, governs the will so that it does not will more than what it is fitting and expedient for it to will, is something?

S: No sensible person will think that it is nothing.

T: This, as I believe you fully realize, is nothing other than justice.

S: It cannot be thought to be anything else.

T: So it is certain that justice is something.

S: Indeed, it is something outstandingly good.

Chapter 16

That injustice is nothing other than the absence of the justice there ought to be

T: Before it received this justice, was the will obligated to will and to refrain from willing in accordance with justice?

S: The will did not owe[27] what it did not have because it had not received it.

T: But once it had received justice, you have no doubt that it was obligated, unless it were to lose justice by coercion.

S: I think it is always bound by this obligation, whether it retains what it received or spontaneously* abandons it.

T: You're right. But what if the will abandons the justice that was so usefully and so wisely added to it—abandons it without being compelled by any lack or any coercion, but by spontaneously exercising its own power, that is, by willing more than it ought to? Will anything remain in that will besides what we imagined it to have before justice was added to it?

S: Since nothing was added but justice, once justice is lost it is certain that nothing will remain besides what was there before, except that the justice it received made the will a debtor to justice and left behind, as it were, certain beautiful traces of itself when justice was abandoned. For the very fact that it remains a debtor to justice shows that it had been adorned with the nobility of justice. And it is quite just that what has once received justice should always be a debtor to justice, unless it lost justice by coercion. Certainly, if a nature is shown to have once had justice, and to be always obligated to have so noble a good, it is thereby proved to be of far greater dignity than a nature that is known never to have had this good or to have been obligated to have it.

T: You have thought this through very well. But add this to your view: the more praiseworthy a nature that had and ought to have

---

27. Bear in mind that 'ought', 'owe', and 'is obligated' all translate the same Latin word (*debet*). The cognate noun (*debetrix*) is translated 'debtor'.

this good is shown to be, the more blameworthy a person who does not have what he ought is proved to be.

S: I heartily agree.

T: Pinpoint for me what it is in this nature that shows it to be praiseworthy and what makes the person blameworthy.

S: Its having had or being obligated to have justice is what shows the nature's dignity; not having justice is what makes the person corrupt. For his being obligated was brought about by the one who gave him justice, whereas his not having justice was brought about by the one who abandoned justice. After all, he was obligated because he had received it, whereas he does not have it because he forsook it.

T: So what you condemn in the will that did not remain steadfast in justice is not its being a debtor to justice, but its not having justice.

S: What I condemn in it is precisely the absence of justice, or in other words, its not having justice. For as I have already said, its being a debtor to justice confers honor, whereas its not having justice brings disgrace; and the more honorable it is to have justice, the more dishonorable it is to lack justice. Indeed, the only reason that the will is dishonored by not having justice through its own fault is that it is honored by being obligated to have justice by the goodness of its Giver.

T: Don't you judge that a will that does not have the justice it ought to have is unjust, and that there is injustice in it?

S: Who would judge otherwise?

T: I believe you would find nothing in it to condemn if it weren't unjust and there weren't injustice in it.

S: Nothing at all.

T: Therefore, what you condemn in it is nothing other than injustice and its being unjust.

S: I cannot condemn anything else in it.

T: So if, as you just said, you do not condemn anything in it other than the absence of justice and its not having justice, and if it is also true that you do not condemn anything in it other than there being injustice in it, in other words, its being unjust, then clearly its injustice or its being unjust is nothing other than the absence of justice or its not having justice.

S: There's no way there can be any difference between them.

T: Therefore, just as the absence of justice and not having justice have no essence,* so also injustice and being unjust have no being, and therefore they are not something but rather nothing.

S: Nothing could be more logical.

T: Remember also that we've already agreed that once justice has been lost, nothing but the obligation to justice remains in him beyond what he had before he received justice.

S: Right.

T: But before he had justice, he was not unjust and did not have injustice.

S: No.

T: Therefore, either there is no injustice in him and he is not unjust once justice has been lost, or else injustice and being unjust are nothing.

S: No conclusion could be more inevitable.

T: And you conceded that once he has abandoned justice, he has injustice and is unjust.

S: I could hardly fail to realize that!

T: Therefore, his injustice or being-unjust is nothing.

S: You have caused me to know what I used to believe without knowing it.

T: I suppose you also already know why, even though injustice is nothing but the absence of justice and being unjust is nothing but not having justice, it is only after he has abandoned justice and not before he was given it that this absence of justice is called injustice, and not having justice is being unjust, and both are worthy of reproach. The reason is simply this: the absence of justice is dishonorable only where there ought to be justice. For example, not having a beard is not dishonorable for a man who is not yet supposed to have a beard, but once he ought to have a beard, it is unbecoming for him not to have one. In the same way, not having justice is not a defect in a nature that is not obligated to have justice, but it is disgraceful for a nature that ought to have it.[28] And to whatever degree his being supposed to have a beard shows his manly nature, to that degree his not having it disfigures his manly appearance.

S: I now understand quite well that injustice is nothing other than the absence of justice where there ought to be justice.

---

28. "Is not supposed to" and "is not obligated to" both translate *non debet*, which here means "it is not that the case that it ought" rather than "it ought not."

Chapter 17

Why an angel who abandoned justice cannot return to it

T: When we stipulated that only the will for happiness had been given to the angel we discussed earlier, we saw that he could not will anything else.

S: We saw that clearly.

T: Now that he has forsaken justice and retains only the will for happiness that he had before, can the angel who abandoned justice return by his own power to the will for justice, which he could not obtain before it was given to him?

S: Far less so can he return to it now. After all, he could not have justice then because of the way his nature had been created, whereas now he ought not to have it because of his desert and his fault.

T: Then there is no way he can have justice from himself when he doesn't have it, since he cannot have it from himself either before he receives it or after he has abandoned it.

S: He shouldn't have anything from himself.

Chapter 18

In what sense the evil angel made himself unjust and the good made himself just; and that the evil angel owes thanks to God for the goods he received and abandoned, just as the good owes thanks for the goods he received and preserved

T: Isn't there a sense in which, when he had justice, he was able to give himself justice?

S: How could he do that?

T: We use the word 'make' in many ways. For example, we say that we "make" something when we make a thing exist, and also when we can make it not exist but we refrain from doing so. And in this latter way he was able to give himself justice, since he was able to take it away from himself and also able not to take it away. In the same way, the one who remained steadfast in the truth in which he was made did not make himself not have it, although he could have; and thus he both gave himself justice and received all this from God. For both angels received from God the having of justice, the ability to retain justice, and the ability to abandon it. God gave them this last ability so that they could, in a certain sense, give justice to themselves. For if there was no sense in which they were able to take away justice from themselves, there was also no sense in which they were able to give it to themselves. Therefore, the one who in this sense gave himself justice received from God the very fact that he gave himself justice.

S: I see that they were able to give themselves justice by not taking it away from themselves; but one angel gave it to himself, while another took it away from himself.

T: Then do you see that each ought to give God equal thanks for his goodness, and that the devil is no less obligated to render God his due simply because he took away from himself what God gave him and was unwilling to receive what God offered?

S: I see that.

T: So an evil angel always owes thanks to God for the happiness that he took away from himself, just as a good angel always owes thanks for the happiness that he gave himself.

S: That's quite true.

T: I believe you realize that the only way God can make something unjust is by not making an unjust thing just even though he can. For until someone has received justice, he is neither just nor unjust; and once someone has received justice, he does not become unjust unless he spontaneously* abandons justice. Therefore, just as a good angel made himself just by not taking justice away from himself even though he could, so also God makes an evil angel unjust by not giving justice back to him even though he can.

S: That's easy to see.

Chapter 19

That the will, insofar as it has being, is a good; and that no thing is an evil

T: Let's return to our discussion of the will and recall what we discussed earlier, namely, that before the will receives justice, the will for happiness is not an evil but something good, no matter what it wills. It follows that when it abandons the justice it received, if it is the same essence* it was before, it is something good insofar as it has being; but insofar as the justice that was once in it is no longer there, it is called evil and unjust. For if willing to be like God were evil, the Son of God would not will to be like the Father; and if willing the lowest pleasures were evil, the will of brute animals would be called evil. But the will of the Son of God is not evil, since it is just; and the will of an irrational animal is not called evil, since it is not unjust.

Hence, it follows that no will is an evil;[29] on the contrary, every will is a good insofar as it has being, since it is the work of God, and it is evil only insofar as it is unjust. Now only two sorts of things are called evil: an evil will, and whatever is called evil on account of an evil will (for example, an evil human being or an evil action); therefore, nothing is more evident than that no thing is an evil. Evil is nothing other than the absence of justice that has been forsaken, either in a will or in some other thing on account of an evil will.

Chapter 20

In what sense God makes both evil wills and evil actions; and in what sense they are received from him

S: Your disputation is constructed out of such true, necessary, and evident arguments that I would see no argument that could undermine it, except that I find it entails something I think should not be said, and I cannot see how that conclusion could fail to be true if what you say is also true. For if willing to be like God is not nothing or evil, but something good, it could be had only from him from whom comes everything that is. Therefore, if an angel did not have anything he did not receive, then whatever he had, he received from the one from whom he had it. But what did he receive from God that God did not give? Therefore, if he had the will to be like God, he had it because God gave it to him.

T: How would it be surprising if we acknowledge that God gives an evil will by not preventing it even though he can—especially since the power to will anything at all is from him alone—in the same way in which God is said to lead us into temptation when he does not free us from it?

S: Looked at in that way, it doesn't seem absurd.

---

29. Notice, Anselm does not say that no will is evil (*nullam voluntatem esse malam*), since obviously the devil's will is evil. He says that no will is *an* evil (*nullam voluntatem esse malum*); that is, every will, insofar as it has being, is a good.

T: Now it is not unusual for us to speak of giving not only when someone spontaneously* hands something over but also when someone grudgingly lets it go. So if there is no giving without receiving, it is also not incongruous for us to speak of receiving not only when someone accepts what has been handed over but also when someone presumes to take what is unlawful.

S: What you say strikes me as neither incongruous nor unusual.

T: Then suppose we say that when the devil willed what he ought not, he both received this from God, since God permitted it, and did not receive it from God, since God did not consent. How would this be contrary to the truth?

S: Nothing in that statement seems incompatible with the truth.

T: So when the devil turned his will to what he ought not, both that willing and that turning were something, and nonetheless he had this something from no source other than God, since he could neither will anything nor move his will unless permitted by God, who makes all natures, substantial* and accidental,* universal and individual. For insofar as the will and the turning or movement of the will is something, it is good and is from God. But insofar as the will lacks justice, which it ought not to be without, it is not an unqualified* evil, but something evil; and its being evil is not from God, but from the one who wills or moves his will. Injustice, after all, is an unqualified evil, since it is nothing other than evil, which is nothing. By contrast, the nature in which there is injustice is something evil, since it is something, and something distinct from injustice, which is evil and nothing. Therefore, that which is something is brought about by God and is from God, but that which is nothing, i.e., evil, is brought about by the unjust person and is from him.

S: Certainly we have to acknowledge that God brings about the natures of all things. But who would grant that he brings about the individual actions of perverse wills or the depraved movement of the will by which an evil will moves itself?

T: What's so surprising about our saying that God brings about the individual actions that are brought about by an evil will, since we acknowledge that he brings about the individual substances that are brought about by an unjust will and a dishonorable action?

S: I have no objection to make. I can't deny that any given action is genuinely something, and I refuse to say that anything that genuinely has some essence* is not brought about by God. And this argument of yours in no way accuses God or excuses the devil; in fact, it completely excuses God and accuses the devil.

Chapter 21
That the evil angel could not foreknow that he was going to fall

But I would like to know whether the rebel angel foreknew that he was going to abandon justice.

T: When you ask whether the angel who did not remain steadfast in the truth foreknew that he was going to fall, it's important to distinguish what sort of knowledge you mean. If you're asking about the knowledge that exists only when something is understood through a conclusive argument, then I reply emphatically that what can fail to be the case cannot be known, since what can fail to be the case cannot be shown by any conclusive argument to be the case. So it is clear that there was no way he could foreknow his own fall, which was not necessarily going to happen. After all, suppose this fall was not going to happen. Do you think he could have foreknown it if it was not going to happen?

S: It seems that what can fail to happen in the future cannot be foreknown, and that what is foreknown cannot fail to happen in the future. But I now recall that most celebrated question about divine foreknowledge and free choice. For although it is so authoritatively asserted and so usefully held—so much so that we should in no way doubt it because of any human reasoning—that divine foreknowledge and free choice are compatible with each other, they nonetheless seem to be irreconcilably opposed as far as the reasoning goes by which we examine them. Hence, we see that many people who consider this question are so inclined to one alternative that they entirely abandon the other, dying as they sink beneath the waves of unbelief; many, however, are tossed to and fro as if by opposing winds and are in danger of maintaining contradictory opinions. Therefore, since it is agreed that there is divine foreknowledge of all actions done by free choice and that none of them is a matter of necessity, it still seems that what is foreknown can fail to happen in the future.

T: For the time being I will reply briefly. God's foreknowledge is not properly* called foreknowledge. To him, everything is always present, so he does not have foreknowledge of what is future, but simply knowledge of what is present. So since the argument regarding foreknowledge of a future thing differs from that regarding knowledge of a present thing, divine foreknowledge need not have the same implications as the foreknowledge we are asking about now.

S: I agree.

T: Let's return to the question at hand.

S: I'm happy to do as you say, but on the understanding that when I ask again about the issue I just mentioned, you will not refuse to give me the answer that God will deign to show you. For the resolution of that problem is absolutely crucial, whether someone has already come up with it or will come up with it in the future. I must admit that I have not yet read an argument anywhere that was sufficient for me to understand how the problem is resolved—except in that divine authority that I believe without hesitation.

T: When we come to that question, if we do, we will have whatever success God gives us.[30] For now, however, since the argument given above shows that the fallen angel could not foreknow his fall with the sort of foreknowledge that depends upon a thing's being necessary, listen to another argument that rules out any prior expectation of his fall not only through foreknowledge but even through rational calculation or any suspicion.

S: I am eager to hear it.

T: If, while he was remaining steadfast in his good will, he foreknew that he was going to fall, he either willed that this should happen, or he didn't.

S: One of these must be true.

T: But if, along with his foreknowledge, he at some time had the will to fall, he had already fallen in virtue of that evil will.

S: What you say is evident.

T: So it's not the case that before his fall he knew he was going to fall and also willed to fall.

S: No objection can be raised against your conclusion.

T: But if he foreknew he was going to fall and did *not* will it, then the more he willed to remain steadfast, the more his distress made him wretched.

S: That can't be denied.

T: And the more he willed to remain steadfast, the more just he was; and the more just he was, the happier he deserved to be.

S: Undeniably so.

---

30. Anselm takes up the issue at length in *De concordia*.

T: Therefore, if he knew he was going to fall but did not will his fall, then the happier he deserved to be, the more wretched he actually was—and that's absurd.

S: I can't deny that that follows, but we often recognize that this happens not only without any absurdity but even in a praiseworthy way and through heavenly grace. For often—if I may mention a few things about the sufferings of the just—the more just someone is, the more he is moved by compassion for the plight of another. And we often see that someone who is more steadfast in justice is more brutally persecuted by the unjust.

T: The case is not the same for human beings as it is for that angel. The nature of human beings has now been made capable of suffering countless misfortunes because of the sin of our first parent, and out of this capacity for suffering, grace works incorruptibility for us in many ways. The angel, by contrast, had not yet deserved to suffer any evil because of some previous sin.

S: You have met my objection. It is obvious that this argument not only denies the evil angel foreknowledge of his fall but also eliminates any opinion that he was going to fall.

T: And there is something else that I think shows convincingly that he did not in any way conceive his future sin beforehand. Certainly he would have conceived it as either coerced or spontaneous.* Now he would not have supposed there was anything that might ever coerce him, and as long as he willed to persevere in the truth, he could in no way think he was going to abandon it by his will alone. For it has already been shown that as long as he had an upright will, he willed to persevere in that will. Therefore, as long as he willed to persevere in retaining what he had, I can't see any way he could have so much as suspected that he was going to abandon it by his will alone, without any additional cause playing a role. I don't deny that he knew he could change the will that he was retaining. I just mean that he could not have thought that, with no other cause acting upon him, he would ever spontaneously change the will that he willed to persevere in retaining.

S: Anyone who attentively understands what you are saying will see clearly that the evil angel could in no way know or think that he was going to do the evil act that he did.

Chapter 22

That he knew he ought not to will that which he sinned by willing, and that he knew he deserved punishment if he sinned

But I also want you to show whether he knew he ought not to will that which he willed when he sinned.

T: You shouldn't be in doubt about that if you think through what was said earlier. For if he hadn't known that he ought not to will that which he unjustly willed, he wouldn't have been aware that he ought to retain the will that he abandoned. And so he would not have been just by retaining, or unjust by abandoning, the justice that he would not have known. In fact, if he didn't know that he ought to be content with what he had received, he also could not have refrained from willing to have more than he had. And finally, since he was so rational that nothing prevented him from making use of reason, he was not ignorant of what he ought to will and what he ought not to will.

S: I don't see how your argument can be refuted, but even so, it seems to me that it prompts a certain question: if he knew that he ought not to abandon what he had received, surely he knew equally well that he would deserve punishment if he abandoned it. How, then, could someone who had received an incliminable will for happiness spontaneously* will that which would bring him wretchedness?

Chapter 23

That he should not have known that he would be punished if he sinned

T: Just as it is certain that he must have known he would deserve punishment if he sinned, so also he should not have known that he would be punished if he sinned.

S: How did he not know that, if he was so rational that his rationality was not prevented from knowing the truth, as ours is often prevented by the burden of this corruptible body?

T: Because he was rational, he was able to understand that it would be just for him to be punished if he sinned. But since God's "judgments are a great abyss" [Psalm 36:6] and "his ways are unsearchable" [Romans 11:33], the angel could not have known for certain whether God would in fact do what he could justly do. Suppose someone were to say this: "There is no way the angel could have believed that God would damn his own creature, which he had made out of his great goodness, because of the creature's fault—especially since there had been no example of avenging justice prior to the angel's injustice. And he would have been certain that God had so wisely established the number of those who were meant to enjoy him that, just as it contained nothing superfluous, so also it would have been incomplete if it had been reduced. He would have been certain, too, that so outstanding a work of God would not remain incomplete in any part. If human beings had already been created, he could not have known by any reasoning that God was going to substitute human nature for the angelic or angelic nature for the human if either fell, instead of each nature's being restored to the state in which it was created, to fill its own proper place and not that of another. Or, if human beings had not yet been created, far less could he have thought they were going to be created as a substitute for another nature." If someone were to say all this, is there anything unreasonable in it?

S: To me it seems reasonable rather than unreasonable.

T: Let's return to what I had said, namely, that he should not have had this knowledge, since if he had known this, he, as one who both willed and had happiness, could not have spontaneously willed that which would make him wretched. Therefore, he would not have been just for not willing what he ought not, since he would not have been able to will it.

Now consider another argument about whether he should have had the knowledge you're asking about. If he had known he would be punished, either he would have sinned or he wouldn't.

S: One of those would have been the case.

T: If he sinned even though he had foreseen such punishment, and even though he lacked nothing and there was nothing compelling him, he would be that much more deserving of punishment.

S: Yes.

T: So this foreknowledge was not beneficial for him.

S: Indeed, foreknowing his punishment was not beneficial for one who was going to sin.

T: Now if he hadn't sinned, he would have refrained from sinning either by his good will alone, or out of fear of punishment.

S: There's no other possibility.

T: But he showed by his action that he would not have refrained from sinning solely out of love for justice.

S: Undoubtedly.

T: But if he had refrained from sinning out of fear, he would not be just.

S: It is clear that he should not have known at all that the punishment now inflicted upon him was going to follow his sin.

Chapter 24

That even the good angel should not have known this

Now we believe that both the angel who remained steadfast in the truth and the angel who did not were endowed with equal knowledge when first created. But I don't see why this knowledge was denied to the angel whose good will was so tenacious that it was sufficient for him to refrain from sinning.

T: Still, if he had foreknown this punishment, he neither could have nor should have disregarded it.

S: So it seems.

T: Therefore, just as the love of justice was sufficient by itself for him not to sin, so also his hatred of that punishment would have been sufficient by itself for him not to sin.

S: Nothing could be clearer.

T: So there would have been two causes of his not sinning: one honorable and useful, the other not honorable and useless: that is, the love of justice and the hatred of punishment. For it is not honorable not to sin solely out of hatred of punishment, and hatred of punishment is useless for not sinning in a case where the love of justice is sufficient by itself.

S: There's no objection I could raise.

T: Then isn't his perseverance more resplendently satisfactory when only one cause of that perseverance is seen in him, a cause that is both useful and honorable because it is spontaneous,* than if at the same time another cause were to present itself, one that is useless and dishonorable because it is understood to be necessary?*

S: What you are saying is so evident that I am now glad he didn't know what a little while ago I wanted him to have known—except that we can't deny he has that knowledge now, since thanks to the example of the angel who sinned he can't help having it.

Chapter 25

That even if the good angel is said to be no longer
able to sin solely because he now has this knowledge
because of the fall of the devil, this is to his glory

T: Although both the good and the evil angel are now certain that
such a fault will be followed by such punishment, this knowledge
is different in each, the cause of the knowledge is not the same,
and its result is different. For what the evil angel knows by his
own experience, the good angel learned solely by someone else's
example. The evil angel knows it by one means, because he did
not persevere; the good angel knows it by another means, because
he did persevere. Hence, just as the evil angel's knowledge is to
his discredit, since his not persevering was blameworthy, so also
the good angel's knowledge is to his glory, since his persevering
was praiseworthy. So if the good angel is said to be no longer able
to sin solely because he has this knowledge, it is perfectly clear
that just as the knowledge itself, which was acquired by his
praiseworthy perseverance, is glorious, so also the inability to sin
that arises out of that glorious knowledge is to his glory. Therefore,
just as the evil angel deserves reproach for being unable to return
to justice, so also the good angel deserves praise for being unable
to desert justice. For just as the evil angel cannot now return to
justice because he deserted it by his evil will alone, so also the
good angel is no longer able to desert justice because he remained
in it by his good will alone. So it is clear that just as the evil
angel's punishment for sin is his inability to recover what he
abandoned, so also the good angel's reward for justice is his
inability to abandon what he retained.

S: Your discussion of the good angel's knowledge and his inability to sin would be very appealing—if, as you say, it is because he persevered that the good angel comes to have this
knowledge and the inability to sin. But in fact it seems that he
acquired them, not because he persevered, but because the rebel
angel did not persevere.

T: If you're right, the good angel can rejoice over the fall of the
rebel angel inasmuch as it was beneficial for him that the evil angel fell, since he acquired this knowledge—in virtue of which he
can no longer sin or be wretched—not because of his own good
deserts, but because of someone else's evil deserts. And all of that
is wildly absurd.

S: The more absurd it seems—as you point out—that the fall of the sinful angel was advantageous for the angel who remained steadfast, the more necessary it is for you to show that the good angel did not receive the knowledge in question because the evil angel sinned.

T: You must not say that the good angel attained this knowledge because the evil one sinned, but rather that he attained this knowledge *through the example of the fallen angel* because the evil angel sinned. For if neither had sinned, God would have given both the same knowledge by some other means because of the merit of their perseverance, without the example of anyone's fall. After all, no one will say that God could not have given his angels this knowledge by some other means. Therefore, since the evil angel sinned, God used his example to teach the good angel what he was going to teach anyway: not on account of some lack of power, because he could not teach it in any other way, but through that greater power of his through which he was able to bring good out of evil, so that no evil would remain disordered in the realm of all-powerful wisdom.

S: What you say is very appealing.

T: And so it is evident that even if the good angel were no longer able to sin solely because he knows that the sin of the evil angel was met with punishment, even so, this inability would not diminish his praiseworthiness but would be the reward for his having preserved justice. But you know, because it became clear earlier,[31] that the reason he cannot sin is that by the merit of his perseverance he has come to the point where he no longer sees what more he could will.

S: I haven't forgotten any of what we found out earlier through the investigations of reason.

Chapter 26

*What it is we fear when we hear the word 'evil',
and what causes the deeds that injustice is said
to cause, given that injustice and evil are nothing*

But even though you have answered all my questions, there is something else I'm eager for you to explain. Since evil is nothing, what is it we fear when we hear the word 'evil'? And what causes

---

31. In chapter 6.

the deeds that injustice, which is an evil, seems to cause, for example, in a robber or a lustful person?

T: I will answer you briefly. The evil that is injustice is always nothing; but the evil that is misfortune is undoubtedly sometimes nothing, as in the case of blindness, and sometimes something, as in the case of sadness and pain. And we always hate the misfortune that is something. So when we hear the word 'evil', we do not fear the evil that is nothing, but the evil that is something, which follows from the absence of good. For many misfortunes that are evil and are something follow from injustice and blindness, which are evil and are nothing; and it is the former that we fear when we hear the word 'evil'.

Now when we say that injustice causes robbery, or that blindness causes someone to fall into a ditch, we must in no way understand this to mean that injustice or blindness causes something; rather, it means that if there had been justice in the will and sight in the eyes, neither the robbery nor the fall into the ditch would have happened. It's like when we say that the absence of the rudder drives the ship into the rocks or that the absence of the reins causes the horse to run wild; that simply means that if there had been a rudder on the ship and reins for the horse, the winds would not have driven the ship and the horse would not have run wild. For in the same way that a ship is controlled by the rudder and a horse by the reins, the human will is governed by justice and the feet by vision.

S: You have so thoroughly put my mind at rest concerning the evil that is injustice that every difficulty about it that used to trouble me has been cleared up. For this evil seems to generate a difficulty: if it were an essence,* it would be from God, since it is necessary that whatever is something is from him, and it is impossible that sin or injustice be from him. But I see that there is nothing threatening to a correct faith if the evil that is misfortune should sometimes be something.

Chapter 27

From what source evil entered the angel
who used to be good

But don't grow weary of giving brief answers to my foolish questions, so that I might know how to answer those who ask the same thing. After all, it's not always easy to respond wisely to someone who asks a foolish question. So I ask this: from what source did the evil that is called injustice or sin first enter the angel who had been created just?

T: You tell me: from what source does nothing enter something?

S: Nothing neither enters nor goes away.

T: Then why do you ask from what source injustice entered, given that injustice is nothing?

S: Because when justice departs from where it was, we say that injustice comes in.

T: Then use the clearer and more proper* expression, and ask about the departure of justice. For often an apt question makes for an easier answer, while an inept question makes the answer more difficult.

S: Then why did justice depart from the just angel?

T: If you want to speak properly, justice did not depart from the angel; rather, the angel abandoned justice by willing what he ought not to will.

S: Why did he abandon justice?

T: In saying that he abandoned it by willing what he ought not, I indicate clearly both why and how he abandoned it. He abandoned justice *because* he willed what he ought not to will, and he abandoned it *by* willing what he ought not to will.

S: Why did he will what he ought not?

T: No cause preceded this will, except that he was able to will.

S: Did he will it because he was able to will it?

T: No, because the good angel was likewise able to will it, but he didn't. No one wills what he can will simply because he can, with no other cause, although no one ever wills anything unless he can will it.

S: Then why did he will it?

T: Simply because he willed it. For there was no other cause by which his will was in any way incited or attracted. Instead, his will was its own efficient cause, if I may put the matter that way, and its own effect.

Chapter 28

That the power to will what he ought not was always good,
and that willing itself is good with respect to its essence

S: If that power to will, and the willing itself, were something,
they were good and were from God.

T: Both were something. The power indeed was something
good, a spontaneous* gift of God, whereas the willing was good
according to its essence* but bad in that it was done unjustly—
and yet it was from God, since whatever is something comes from
God. Indeed, any given person has from God not only what God
spontaneously gives him, but also what he steals unjustly with
God's permission. And just as God is said to do what he permits
to be done, so also he is said to give what he permits to be stolen.
Therefore, since it was with God's permission that the angel stole
his exercise of the power God had spontaneously given him, he
had this exercise of power—which is nothing other than the willing itself—from God. For willing is nothing other than exercising
the power to will, just as speaking is nothing other than exercising the power to speak.[32]

---

32. See Appendix B.

APPENDIX A

Proslogion 8

*How God is both merciful and impassible**

But how are you both merciful and impassible? For if you are impassible, you do not feel compassion, and if you do not feel compassion, your heart is not sorrowful out of compassion for sorrow; and that is what being merciful is.[1] But if you are not merciful, how is it that you are such a comfort to the sorrowful?

So how, Lord, are you both merciful and not merciful? Is it not because you are merciful in relation to us but not in relation to yourself? You are indeed merciful according to what we feel, but not according to what you feel. For when you look with favor upon us in our sorrow, we feel the effect [*effectum*] of your mercy, but you do not feel the emotion [*affectum*] of mercy. So you are merciful, because you save the sorrowful and spare those who sin against you; but you are also not merciful, because you are not afflicted with any feeling of compassion for sorrow.

---

1. In Latin, "sorrowful heart" is *miserum cor*; 'merciful' is *misericors*.

APPENDIX B

On the Harmony of Divine Foreknowledge,
Predestination, and Grace with Free Choice
(De concordia)

Question 3, Chapter 11

Now 'to will' is equivocal in the same way that 'to see' is. After all, both one who is making use of vision and one who is not, but has an aptitude for seeing, are said to see. In the same way, both one who is making use of the instrument for willing by intending what he wills, and one who is not making use of it but has an affection (that is, an aptitude) for willing, are said to will.

One can thereby recognize that there is a distinction between the will that is the instrument for willing, the will that is the affection of that instrument, and the will that is the actual exercise of that instrument. For if we affirm that a just man, even when he is asleep or not thinking about anything in particular, has the will to live justly, while we deny that an unjust man, when he is asleep, has the will to live justly, we are ascribing to the just man the very same will that we deny of the unjust man. It is clear, however, that when we say of the sleeping unjust man that he does not have the will to live justly, we are not denying that he has the will I have called the instrument for willing; for all human beings always have that will, whether they are awake or asleep. Therefore, since the will that we thus affirm to be in the good man is the very same will that we deny is in the bad man, our claim does not signify that the good man has the will that is the instrument for willing, but that he has the will by which that instrument is affected. For it's perfectly clear that the will that is the exercise of that instrument is not present in someone who is asleep, unless he is dreaming. So when we say that the will to live justly is present in someone who is asleep, we don't mean the will that is the exercise of the instrument for willing. Therefore, the will that is an affection is neither the will that is an instrument nor the will that is the exercise of that instrument. Furthermore, everyone realizes that the will that is the instrument for willing is distinct from the will that is its exercise, since if I say that I do not have the will to write, no one understands me to mean that I don't have the instrument for willing to write. So 'will' has three distinct senses: instrument, affection, and exercise.

Appendix C

Proslogion 7

In what sense God is omnipotent even though there are many things he cannot do

But how are you omnipotent if you cannot do everything?[1] And how can you do everything if you cannot be corrupted, or lie, or cause what is true to be false (as, for example, to cause what has been done not to have been done), or many other such things?

Or is the ability to do these things not power but weakness? For someone who can do these things can do what is not beneficial to himself and what he ought not to do. And the more he can do these things, the more power misfortune and wickedness have over him, and the less he has over them. So whoever can do these things can do them, not in virtue of his power, but in virtue of his weakness. So when we say that he "can" do these things, it is not because he has the power to do them, but because his weakness gives something else power over him. Or else it is some other manner of speaking, such as we often use in speaking loosely. For example, we sometimes say 'to be' instead of 'not to be', or 'to do' instead of 'not to do' or 'to do nothing'. For often when someone denies that something exists, we say "It is as you say it is"; but it would seem more correct to say "It is not as you say it is not." Again, we say "This man is sitting just as that man is doing" or "This man is resting just as that man is doing"; but to sit is not to do anything, and to rest is to do nothing. In the same

---

1. This chapter is full of wordplay in the Latin that does not all come across in English. The words for 'power' (*potentia*), 'weakness' (*impotentia*), and various forms of the verb 'can' (*posse*)—also translated here as 'have power'—all share a common stem. And the word for omnipotent (*omnipotens*) means literally "able to do everything" (*omnia potens*).

way, then, when someone is said to have the "power" to do or suffer something that is not beneficial to himself or that he ought not to do, by 'power' we really mean 'weakness'. For the more he has this "power," the more power misfortune and wickedness have over him, and the less he has over them. Therefore, Lord God, you are all the more truly omnipotent because you can do nothing through weakness, and nothing has power over you.

GLOSSARY

References are given using abbreviations of the Latin titles, followed by the chapter number, as follows:

DV = On Truth (De veritate)
DLA = On Freedom of Choice (De libertate arbitrii)
DCD = On the Fall of the Devil (De casu diaboli)

accident   An accident is a feature something has that does not belong to its essence* (in sense 3).

accidental (nature)   An accidental nature is simply an accident.

accidentally   If two things have the same essence but differ from each other in some way, they are said to differ accidentally. For example, two human beings differ accidentally, since they have the same essence but differ in their accidents*; a human being and a cat differ substantially,* since they have different essences.

body   The word 'body' is used more broadly in philosophy than in ordinary language. Any material object at all is a body in the philosophical sense. (Similarly, in scientific language we might speak of "a body in motion.") So chairs and tables are bodies, as are the bodies of human beings and other living creatures.

difference   In a definition, the difference is what sets apart one sort of thing from others in the same genus.* For example, in the definition of human being as "rational animal," *rational* is the difference that sets human beings apart from other things in the genus* *animal.*

essence (Latin, *essentia*)   Anselm uses the word *'essentia'* in a variety of ways:

1. It signifies the individual thing that exists. In this usage "an essence" is synonymous with "an existent being."

2. Sometimes it is used to indicate what a present-day philosopher might call "ontological status." In this sense one might say that darkness, for example, has no essence, because it is nothing more than the absence of light, whereas light has essence because it is something in its

106

own right. To say that darkness has no essence, in this sense, is therefore equivalent to saying that it is nothing and that it is not something.

3. It sometimes signifies the nature of a thing. For example, the essence of a human being is to be rational, animal, and mortal. Such other features as being tall or short, dark or fair, male or female are accidents.*

4. Occasionally Anselm uses it strictly as the abstract noun corresponding to *esse*, "to be," where that verb includes the meanings "exists" and "is a certain way." In such cases I translate *'essentia'* as 'being', and 'being' should be understood to include the meanings 'existence' and 'being a certain way'.

genus   In a definition, the genus* is the general classification to which the thing defined belongs. For example, in the definition of human being as "rational animal," *animal* is the genus* to which human beings belong. (See also difference.*)

impassible   This word comes from the Latin *'pati'*, "to undergo or suffer," which is contrasted with *'agere'*, "to do or act." To say that God is impassible therefore means that he cannot suffer or undergo anything. He cannot be acted upon by anything else; he simply acts.

improperly   A word is used improperly when it is used in a way that is misleading or not philosophically precise. Anselm is concerned in particular about expressions that, if taken literally, seem to attribute a power, obligation, or characteristic to something that does not actually have that power, obligation, or characteristic. For example, if I say "Elderly parents ought to be supported by their children," I seem to be attributing an obligation to the parents. But in fact it is the children who have an obligation, the obligation to support their parents; so Anselm would say that I am using the word 'ought' improperly.

imputed   An act is imputed to an agent whenever the agent is held to be both causally and morally responsible for the act.

natural/naturally   An act is natural (or someone acts naturally) when the act can be fully explained by the nature God gave the agent.

nature   Nature is interchangeable with essence* in senses 1, 2, and 3.

necessary   A proposition is necessary (or necessarily true) if it is not possible for that proposition to be false. An action is necessary if it is not spontaneous.*

necessity   An action is said to happen out of necessity if it is not done spontaneously.*

prior (in nature) x is prior in nature to y if and only if x explains, accounts for, or causes y. Priority in nature does not imply priority in time, as Anselm argues in *DV* 12.

properly   A word is used properly when it is used strictly and literally, not loosely or in a way that is apt to be misleading or violates precise philosophical usage. In *DV* 12 Anselm says that nothing, or hardly anything, can be said of God properly.

several   I sometimes use 'several' to translate the Latin word *'plures'*, which means "more than one." The reader should therefore keep in mind that 'several' need not imply a large number; it simply implies more than one.

simple   To say that God is simple is to say that he has no parts. More specifically, Anselm argues that God has no spatial parts, no temporal parts, and no metaphysical parts.

spontaneous(ly)   It is crucial to understand that spontaneous and spontaneously are used as technical terms in this translation to represent the Latin *spontaneus* and *sponte*, for which there are no good English equivalents; they do not connote impulsiveness or lack of premeditation, as they do in ordinary usage. In this technical sense, an act is spontaneous (or an agent acts spontaneously) when the act can be fully explained only by reference to something that originates within the agent. For example, Anselm argues in *DCD* that the sin of the angels was spontaneous, because it was up to them whether to sin or not; the powers and the knowledge they had received from God were not enough to explain either their sinning or their remaining just. If an act is not spontaneous, it is natural.*

substance   A substance is the individual thing that exists, as distinguished from some part or feature of the individual.

substantial (nature)   A substantial nature is simply a substance.

substantially   Two things differ substantially when they have a different essence* (in sense 3). For example, a dog and a horse differ substantially, whereas two horses differ only accidentally.*

unqualified (Latin, *simplex*)   An unqualified evil is something that is evil, period. A qualified evil is something that is evil in a certain respect or to a certain degree.

INDEX